# THE MAN
# FROM
# MARS HILL

## THE LIFE AND TIMES OF
## T.B. LARIMORE

# J.M. POWELL

21st Century Christian
2809 12th Avenue South
Nashville, TN 37204

# ACKNOWLEDGMENTS

Special thanks to Dr. Sue Berry, professor emeritus of English at David Lipscomb University, for editorial review, Maxine Brown for typography, and Cathy Brown for typesetting and layout.

Pictures of T.B. Larimore, his family and home were generously provided by Mars Hill Bible School in Florence, Alabama.

# DEDICATION

A well known T.B. Larimore scholar, Basil Overton lives in Florence, Alabama some four miles from "Mars Hill" where Larimore resided and operated a school for preachers. This he did for about eighteen years.

In this school—Mars Hill College—Larimore trained scores of gospel preachers. Larimore was a profound scholar and natural born teacher. In 1889, F.D. Srygley wrote a book called *Larimore and His Boys.* Srygley dedicated his book "to all the boys who love their mothers and the Lord and strive to be educated and useful." After reading *Larimore and His Boys*, J. W. McGarvey referred to it as "one of the most inspirational books I have ever read." Basil Overton has taken on much of the spirit of Larimore in his own personal life. Being vitally connected with Heritage University in Florence, Overton is doing much to educate young men to be "faithful preachers" of the word.

Overton is also the editor of *World Evangelist*, one of the most widely circulated periodicals published by members of the churches of Christ. Overton often publishes articles about Larimore's life and works.

J.M. Powell
October 18, 2001

# CONTENTS

DEDICATION .................................................................... V

FOREWORD ....................................................................... 9

PREFACE ........................................................................... 15

CHAPTER 1—HISTORICAL BACKGROUND .................... 19

CHAPTER 2—BRIGHT PROMISES:

    T.B. LARIMORE'S EARLY YEARS .............................. 33

CHAPTER 3—MATURE YEARS: FAMILY TIES ............. 47

CHAPTER 4—MARVELOUS MEETINGS ....................... 59

CHAPTER 5—A MAN OF PEACE AND PURITY ........... 87

CHAPTER 6—HIS LATER YEARS ............................... 105

CHAPTER 7—CONTEMPORARY APPRAISALS

    OF T.B. LARIMORE .................................................. 123

CONCLUSION ................................................................ 141

SERMONS OF T.B. LARIMORE ................................... 145

ENDNOTES .................................................................... 185

BIBLIOGRAPHY ............................................................. 193

# FOREWORD

It is altogether proper that James Marvin
Powell, evangelist, educator, and church historian
wrote this book about the saintly Theophilus Brown
Larimore who was also an evangelist and an educator of extraordinary ability. It has been my pleasure
to know and admire J.M. Powell nearly half a century. He and his wife, the former Mildred Cliett, were
married in 1935 and they live in Nashville, Tennessee.
I was very gratified to write and publish in the
August 1997 issue of *The World Evangelist*, "A Tribute
to J.M. (Marvin) and Mildred Powell."

## EDUCATION

Marvin was born March 12, 1907 in
Senatobia, Mississippi. He is well-educated. He

has the following degrees: A.A., David Lipscomb College; B.A., Oglethorpe University; M.A., Harding Graduate School; and L.L.D., Lubbock Christian College. He was President and faculty member of Ohio Valley College in Parkersburg, West Virginia for four years in the 1960's. It was my pleasure to present five lectures on "The Life And Work Of Alexander Campbell" at that college while Marvin was President.

PREACHING CAREER

J.M. began his preaching career at Cedar Grove church of Christ in Nashville, Tennessee in 1927. He had become a Christian before that when A.H. Smith baptized him into Christ. Marvin was the regular preacher for many churches of Christ, including: East Hill in Pensacola, Florida; Bardstown Road in Louisville, Kentucky; Druid Hills in Atlanta, Georgia; the Fourth Avenue church in Franklin, Tennessee; Jackson Avenue in Memphis, Tennessee; and Central in Chattanooga, Tennessee.

SCHOLAR IN HISTORY OF THE RESTORATION MOVEMENT

Dr. Powell is an outstanding scholar in the history of the Restoration Movement, which is a movement based on the plea to go to the New Testament and learn and practice the ancient order of matters in religion and just be Christians or members of the church we read about in that book!

Some have said this cannot be done, but they are very wrong, for multitudes have done it!

Dr. Powell has lectured on the Restoration Church History across this country, and in London, Birmingham, and Liverpool in England, and in Glasgow and Edinburgh in Scotland, and in Belfast, Northern Ireland. He has researched the roots of the Restoration Movement in England, Northern Ireland, Scotland and New England. He owns a sizeable collection of rare Restoration materials. He is a member of the Tennessee Historical Society.

BOOKS AUTHORED

N. B. Hardeman's daughter, Mary Nelle Powers, and Marvin Powell wrote a book of about 400 pages about brother Hardeman entitled: *N.B.H.: A Biography of Nicholas Brodie Hardeman*. (I was greatly blessed by having Mary Nelle as my grammar teacher and her father as one of my greatest teachers at Freed-Hardeman College.)

Dr. Powell also wrote *A History Of The Franklin, Tennessee church of Christ.*

Another book by Dr. Powell is entitled, *The Cause We Plead: A Story Of The Restoration Movement.*

Marvin has also written for several gospel journals.

MY CONNECTIONS WITH THE LARIMORE FAMILY

When T.B. Larimore died March 18, 1929, I was four years old. I regret I did not know him. I have read a lot about him and have admired him very much. I do not mean that I agree with everything he said, but I recognize him as having been a very capable and sincere man. He was an orator in the truest sense. Someone said an orator is one who makes you see with your ears! Someone else said eloquence is the power to translate a truth into language perfectly intelligible to the person to whom you speak.

I have been to the gravesite of T.B. Larimore's grandmother, Mary Larimore, in the Sequatchie Valley of Tennessee. I have been to the site where the house stood in which T.B. Larimore lived when he was a boy in Dunlap, Tennessee. I have been to the grave of his mother, Nancy, at Stantonville, Tennessee. She died September 2, 1902, and N.B. Hardeman preached her funeral.

In 1958, my son Timothy (1947-1974) and I lived a week with T.B. Larimore's son Virgil and his wife Exie, while I preached in a series of meetings for the Mars Hill church of Christ in Florence, Alabama where T.B. Larimore preached so much, including about 30 series of gospel meetings in which he preached there. My Margie and I have been members of the Mars Hill church about twelve years.

During that in week in Virgil's home, I was reading *Larimore And His Boys* by F.D. Syrgley. Virgil "filled me in" on several matters of interest about his daddy. One thing he told me was, "I do not understand how my daddy did so much."

Virgil also took me to visit with his sister, Dedie Larimore George, who lived near Florence. Many years later I spoke at the funeral of Julia George, a daughter of Dedie and her husband James. We conducted the funeral in the family cemetery on the George farm. Dedie and James' grandson, Jim Walden, is one of my friends. He is one of T.B. Larimore's great grandsons.

Basil Overton, Evangelist
Editor of *The World Evangelist*
Florence, Alabama
October 18, 2001

The Larimores
(back row) Dedie, Toppie, Virgil, Ettie
(front row) Granville, Esther, T.B., Herschell

T.B. and Julia Esther Larimore (front row)
with their children and grandchildren

T.B. Larimore and his second wife, Emma Page Larimore

Mars Hill (the Larimore home) in Florence, Alabama

# PREFACE

The purpose for which I have written this book is to show something of the persuasive power of the eloquent, dynamic effective preaching of Theophilos Brown Larimore. Much has been said regarding his winsomeness and popularity, but no effort, to my knowledge, has been made to evaluate and to translate his methods into useful material for the benefit of this and future generations.

It will be the aim of this labor of love to make an analysis of the life and preaching of T.B. Larimore and ascertain the secret of his great success as an evangelist. To accomplish this an attempt is made to discover and record the various elements that made up both his personal life and his sermons.

The purpose of delving deep into the life and methods of T.B. Larimore is to discover the exceptional contributions that he made in the field of gospel preaching. This inquiry goes beyond the impressionistic comments of the newspapers and periodicals, with their "highly colored praise, or blame of, a detail or aspect of speech," to become a sort of judicial type of evaluation.

Secondly, it will provide a clearer picture of why Larimore's preaching was so successful, thereby providing the students of evangelistic preaching the means to readily discern how effective pulpit oratory results from the application of sound theory and principles.

A third and final value that will be provided herein is to be found in the standard of excellence which it helps to put before the reader. This is accomplished when the student observes that the methods of the inimitable Larimore correspond to the principles of speech which he formally mastered, thus reinforcing the desire for excellence of speech. It will be observed by students that Larimore's sermonizing is in perfect agreement with the latest developments of homiletics. It will be seen that he was many years ahead of his time as a preacher. Moreover, it will be observed that though Larimore was not a finished product of any theological seminary, he was indeed and in truth the finished product of the best methods of proclaiming the gospel with telling effect. Since T.B. Larimore was a prominent preacher in the churches of Christ, it was first necessary to obtain the essential background material relative to church development. This entailed special notice of the church, the falling away, the Reformation, and the Restoration Movement. Especially helpful in this particular phase of study were Preserved Smith's *The Age of the Reformation*, and *The Reformation* by Williston Walker, Winfred E. Garrison and Alfred T. DeGroot's *The Disciples of Christ*, *How The Disciples Began and Grew*, by M.M. Davis, and Earle West's *The Search for the Ancient Order*.

It was also necessary to review the background and life of Larimore. Much of the information was derived from *Biographical Sketches of Gospel Preachers*, by H. Leo Boles. Valuable information was secured from *Letters and Sermons of T.B. Larimore*, by F.D. Srygley and Emma Page, who later became Mrs. T.B. Larimore. Use was also made of *Larimore and His Boys*, by F.D. Srygley, and several bound copies of *The Gospel Advocate*. These works in addition to an interview with Virgil Larimore of Florence, Alabama, then the only living son of the distinguished preacher, served as source material. In addition, there were personal interviews with C.E.W. Dorris and S.P. Pittman, both of Nashville, Tennessee, and W. H. Baldy, Jr., a great nephew of Larimore, who lives in Memphis, Tennessee.

## CHAPTER 1

# HISTORICAL BACKGROUND

## THE PRIMITIVE CHURCH

In order to understand a preacher and to evaluate his preaching it is necessary to give the historical background of the movement with which he is identified.

Since the "restoration of primitive Christianity" has been one avowed aim of the movement with which T.B. Larimore was identified, it is necessary to find what primitive Christianity was and how it gradually changed. Since "unity" has been the keynote of the Restoration Movement, it must be noted how the church came to be divided and what efforts have been made: first, to preserve the original unity of the church and second, to restore unity after it has been broken. It may be said in advance that these two ideas—restoration and unity—have a long and colorful history, of which only the high points can be noted.[1]

Some six months before his crucifixion, the Lord said to Simon Peter, "Thou art Peter, and upon this rock I will build my church, and the gates of hades shall not prevail against it."[2] The foundation and the perpetuity of the church are the two fundamental ideas inherent in this passage.

The world was ripe and ready for the coming of Christ and the establishment of the church. The savior appeared in "the fullness of time;"[3] not a moment too soon, not a moment too late. Man often strikes too soon or too late, but not so with God. All things were ready as planned by God and prophesied by the prophets.[4]

The church therefore came into existence on the first Pentecost after the resurrection of Christ.[5] George P. Fisher, the noted church historian, among others, has attested to this fact.[6]

The church of the New Testament was built as the Lord wanted it built. God never intended that man should alter the divinely given pattern in any way. All changes to this divine pattern have been against the authority of God's word. Let us enumerate the distinctive features of the church that Jesus built.

In favor of the oneness and permanence of the church these points should be noted:

1. Christ is the builder or founder of the church of the New Testament. He promised to build but one church, and we have a record of only one church being established by his authority.

2. Christ is the foundation of the New Testament church.[7]

3. Another distinctive feature of the New Testament church is that it has no source of authority save Christ and his word.[8]

4. The names by which the members of the New Testament church are to be known have been designated by God in the divine pattern. In the New Testament, individual members are called "Christians."[9] Collectively, or as a church, they are called by various names, such as "the church of God,"[10] "the churches of Christ,"[11] "the church of the Lord,"[12] "the church,"[13] "the body of Christ,"[14] "the church of the firstborn,"[15] and "the kingdom of the Son of his love."[16]

5. Contrary to the practice of the Jews under the law of Moses, the New Testament church met for worship upon the first day of the week.[17]

6. It is revealed in the New Testament that the church engaged in the following items of worship: (a) The word of God was read.[18] (b) The Lord's Supper was observed in memory of Christ.[19] (c) Its members engaged in prayer.[20] (d) They gave of their means, as the Lord had prospered them.[21] (e) They praised God in song, making melody with the heart.[22]

7. The local churches were independent since each congregation was a unit within itself. The organization of the church consisted simply of elders and deacons in each congregation.[23]

8. The terms of membership in the church were clearly set forth. They were identical with the instructions of Christ in the Great Commission.[24]

9. The unity of organization and practice was a distinctive feature of the New Testament church. Christ had prayed that his followers should be one.[25] Paul had urged that there be no divisions.[26] Repeated warnings had been given to the effect that departures would come.[27]

MEDIEVAL CHRISTIANITY

The organization of the New Testament church was very simple and centered around the local congregation. This organization remained relatively simple, in spite of various departures from the New Testament, until after the conversion of Constantine, when it was patterned after the government of the Roman Empire.[28] Not even the decisions of the councils were regarded as valid until approved by the emperor. Then it was that the local churches were forced to submit to the authority of the councils.

This concentration of power, after a long process, finally culminated in the submission of the church to the authority of the bishop of Rome, who became the pope. In time the hierarchy became so powerful that it wrested control of the church from the government.

When the church was first organized, the elders were the bishops or shepherds of the local congregations. As the church grew and expanded, the office of monarchial bishop arose in each congregation, with the "elders" in submission to the bishop. Thus began a distinction between the office of "bishop" and that of "elder."

From this, the authority was further concentrated until it fell into the hands of "metropolitans" who could dictate to the bishops. Finally the entire control of the church was centralized in the hands of five "Patriarchs" who lived in Constantinople, Rome, Antioch, Alexandria, and Jerusalem. Each ruled one of the five districts which correspond to the four districts of the Roman Empire.

The concentration of power was carried even further, until there arose in the church a supreme head, who corresponded to the one head of political empire. Leo I, then bishop of Rome, claimed supreme leadership and authority over all four patriarchs, but his claims never materialized. Over a century later, the Patriarch of Constantinople tried to get the rank for himself and took the title "Universal Bishop." At this time Gregory I, known as Gregory the Great, became bishop of Rome in A.D. 590, declaring himself the supreme ruler of the church. In the struggle which ensued, the bishop of Rome won out. After this the concentration of power was in Rome. Henceforth the concept of the church continued to be rapidly altered from the simple doctrines of the New Testament into elaborate theological systems and religious creeds.

## REFORMED CHRISTIANITY

Such leaders as John Wycliffe in the fourteenth century and Martin Luther and John Calvin in the early sixteenth century became spokesmen of the unrest that prevailed in Europe. The key thought was protest against the domination of Roman Catholic practices, especially in Germany; and the adherents began to be known as Protestants.[29]

The differing viewpoints of Catholicism and Protestantism are well described by Walker:

> The Reformation vitalized the religious life of Europe; but it divided western Christendom as to the nature of religion itself and of the institutions by which it is propagated. By the Catholic the highest Christian duty was seen in obedience to the infallible voice of a church that claims to be the depository of the truth, the dispenser of sacraments with which alone all certainty of salvation is conjoined, the possessor of a true priesthood of divine appointment—a church characterized by unity expressed in

allegiance to a single earthly head. To the Protestant the profoundest obligations were to use his divinely-given faculties to ascertain for himself, what is the truth of God as contained—so the Reformation age would say—in His infallible and absolutely authoritative word; and to enter through faith into vital, immediate and personal relations with his savior.[30]

The reform movement spread into nearly all parts of Europe, especially within the countries of Germany, Switzerland, England, and Scotland, as well as the Scandinavian countries. Doctrinal differences already divided the great movement into various segments of Lutheran and Calvinistic theology. In this way, several of the presently large Protestant bodies had their beginning. The followers of Luther called themselves Lutherans; the Reformed groups arose; the Anglican church, known later in America as the Protestant Episcopal church, came into being at the decree of Henry VIII; and under John Knox, the Presbyterian church had its beginning in Scotland.

During the seventeenth century, following the Reformation, three distinct influences began to be felt within the Anglican church: the Catholic element, seeking friendliness and reunion with Rome; the Anglican, satisfied with the moderate reforms accomplished under Henry VIII and

Queen Elizabeth; and the separatist individuals and groups who were dissatisfied with both of the former movements.[31] English history during that period is a story of religious intolerance and war among the three forces, while at the same time segments of each were making their way to religious, social, and economic freedom in the new world.[32]

During the first half of the eighteenth century, churches in England and the Colonies, "both established and dissenting, sunk into a state of decline, with formal service, cold, intellectual belief, and a lack of moral power over the population."[33] The situation was made even worse by the low economic and social status of the ministers of religion, whose reputations were generally poor.[34] Furthermore, the frontier conditions in America tended to hamper religious organization, and the influence of Arminianism and rationalism led people away from the formal churches.[35]

## RESTORED CHRISTIANITY

The Reformation Movement of the sixteenth century failed to reform the Catholic church to any appreciable degree. It created, instead, a multiplicity of warring sects. This hostility caused a decline in the spiritual life in northern Europe. Even during his lifetime, Martin Luther noted a serious degeneration in the moral life of the people, and he was greatly distressed by it.[36]

Garrison and DeGroot summarize the condition in this way:

> The Protestant Reformation was a revolt against certain dogmas and practices of the church and against the usurpations and corruptions of the clergy, all of which were characteristic of the medieval system. It was not a rebellion against the church as such, but an attempt to free the church from the bondage which the Roman clergy put upon it...It did not completely succeed in this for two reasons: one was that it developed new and rigid systems of theology which became standards of orthodoxy and grounds of division; the other was that, in establishing state churches and penalizing dissenters, it carried over for a time the medieval idea that conformity must be enforced in order to preserve the security of the state and the stability of the social order as well as the honor of the church.[37]

In this confused and divided religious state, there were numerous individuals who were ceaselessly struggling for a purer religious doctrine and simpler worship, based on the teaching of the New Testament.

These struggles became obvious in various countries. In Germany there was Rupertus

Meldenius, who coined the phrase, "In essentials, unity; in non-essentials, liberty; in all things, charity." In Scotland there was John Drury, who preached in the interest of Christian unity. Hugo Grotius, a Dutch Arminian, pleaded for a return to "the primitive church." Even John Wesley wrote to the Methodists in America in his famous "Christmas letter" (1784) that they "are now at full liberty simply to follow the Scriptures and the primitive church."[38] Time would fail to tell of John Glas, Robert Sandeman, Robert and James Haldane, and a host of others in Europe who were advocating a restoration of New Testament Christianity.

In America there were men in nearly every major Protestant church who were seeking a return to New Testament Christianity. In North Carolina, there was James O'Kelley, Methodist preacher, who became dissatisfied with the polity of the Methodist church. In time he, Rice Haggard, and others broke away and formed the "Christian Church." They were opposed to party and sectarian names. They taught that the Scriptures are "our only creed and rule of faith and practice."[39]

Pleas for New Testament Christianity arose from men in different groups. In New England there were Elias Smith and Dr. Abner Jones, both members of the Baptist church, but were persons more interested in preaching the New Testament than Baptist doctrine as set forth in formal creeds.

These men pled, with telling effect, for a return to New Testament Christianity. In the state of Kentucky around the turn of the century Barton W. Stone, Presbyterian minister, expressed a willingness to accept the Confession of Faith insofar "as I see it consistent with the word of God."[40] It was not long before Thomas Campbell and his illustrious son Alexander, who had a Presbyterian background, set out very vigorously to restore the "Ancient Order of Things."

There were two forceful principles that guided their efforts. The first was their belief that all Christians should be unified, and the second was a conviction that true religious unity must be based upon a common acceptance of the teaching of the Bible. The following excerpt from a sermon by "Raccoon" John Smith of Lexington, Kentucky, in 1832, well describes their position:

> God has but one people on the earth. He has given to them but one Book, and therein exhorts and commands them to be one family. A union such as we plead for—a union of God's people on that one Book—must, then be practicable. Every Christian desires to stand in the whole will of God. The prayer of the Savior, and the whole tenor of his teaching, clearly show that it is God's will that his children should be one. To the Christian, then, such a union must be

desirable. Therefore, the only union practi-
cable or desirable must be based on the
word of God as the only rule of faith and
practice.[41]

In advancing their position, the stalwart
men of the Restoration Movement of the nineteenth century made use of a number of catch slo-
gans which clarified their objectives; e.g., "Back to
the Ancient Order of things;" "No creed but Christ;
no book but the Bible"; "Where the Bible speaks,
we speak; where the Bible is silent we are silent";
and the widely used slogan coined by Rupertus
Meldenius, to which attention has been called.
These men vigorously opposed "man-made"
creeds, which, they contended, led to religious
divisions. They encouraged a conservative inter-
pretation of the Bible and opposed clerical titles of
all kinds.

The movement developed with remarkable
rapidity, so that by 1836 there was a membership of
over one hundred thousand, ranking as the fourth
largest religious group in the United States according to a statement by D.S. Burnett.[42] Alexander
Campbell stated in 1846:

We little suspected, some thirty years
ago, that the principles of Christian union
and a restoration of primitive Christianity in
letter and spirit, in theory and practice,

could have been pled with such success, or have taken such deep hold on the consciences and of the hearts of multitudes of all creeds and parties, of all castes and conditions of society, as we have already lived to witness.[43]

This growth continued to be a source of amazement to the religious forces in America, and in due time T.B. Larimore became a part of this movement, "preaching the word" with phenomenal success.

## CHAPTER II

# BRIGHT PROMISES: T.B. LARIMORE'S EARLY YEARS

Into a religious, philosophical climate ready for such a man as T.B. Larimore was destined to become, he was born.

It was about the middle of the tumultuous nineteenth century—July 10, 1843. Theophilos Brown Larimore came into this world "in rough, rugged, romantic East Tennessee."[1] From the beginning, this setting must have infiltrated the very being of this special one. He invariably spoke of it with love and in typical Larimorean language:

The beautiful Galilee of America, from which lands of fruit and flowers, tall men and towering mountains, fertile fields and limpid streams, have emanated many men of prominence and power.[2]

Little is known of his parents. H. Leo Boles says that "his early advantages were very gloomy and his poverty discouraging, yet through it all he arose to heights of great prominence and service among his fellows upon earth."[3]

F. D. Srygley, his closest friend, quotes a passage from one of Larimore's personal letters, which should satisfy the curiosity of many as to his parentage:

The very best blood, both maternal and paternal, is blended in my veins. I was born in a humble hovel, right where two royal roads of ruined wealth and shattered fortunes met in the shadow of security debts and midnight of the reign of the intoxicating bowl. In other words, my ancestors on both sides were rich, intellectual, influential, successful, and popular. Just as the converging lines came together, some immense security debts had to be paid. There was no shirking. Every dollar was paid; but it took everything....Result—nothing, absolutely nothing left but poverty and honor. Just then I was born—just when the shadows were deepest. Men, hurled from such heights to such depths, turned from these troubles to worse—to strong drink; then the gloom of the darkest night began to gather around my cradle. I can well remember when the yell of the drunken one coming home in the other-wise still hours of night would start all of us from the hut to the woods....We would slip, like little partridges after a scare, back to the gloomy nest....Debt and drunkenness have depressed me to be dejected all my life.[4]

It is no wonder that all who observed him closely went away affected by the down-deep sadness that darkened his countenance. The conviction of the seriousness of his calling only intensified the innate suspicion he had that the joys of life were as illusory as they were fleeting. Only the sweet relationships with his mother and with his family members made life tolerable and tinged it with joy. And the certainty of a home with God and his Son bore him up. This one true Father he had, with all certainty and trust—so much dearer because of his lack on this mortal plain. In 1888 he wrote: "I never knew what it was to have the advice, protection and support of a father."[5]

Larimore was named "Theophilus Brown" because his mother "liked the name, liked the initials—T.B.L.—and because of my blood relationship to the Browns of Tennessee, three of whom were governors of the Volunteer State."[6]

Larimore's boyhood and youth were spent in Sequatchie Valley, Tennessee, near Chattanooga, for his mother moved to this section when he was about nine years old. For this valley he had "an affection that seemed to grow as the years passed by."[7] He referred to it as the "Land of many waters," an idyllic region which "lies between Walden's Ridge and the Cumberland Mountains,...one of the most beautiful valleys in the South."[8]

Wishing to help his mother, whom he tenderly loved, he assumed, at an early age, the responsibility of providing for the family. He hired himself to a farmer for four dollars a month or fifteen and a half cents per day; for that measly sum he did the work of a man as a plow hand. Such hard circumstances, willingly accepted and endured because of love for his mother and sisters, no doubt developed in him the strong, unselfish character that served him well all the days of his life.

Larimore, even as a child, was a private person whose inner needs responded to books. Words and ideas appealed to him and fed a hunger which gnawed beyond the reach of mortal food. He made use of every opportunity to increase his stock of information. He had an intense desire to acquire an education; to this end he studied at home, and by the time he reached his sixteenth year, he had advanced further in study than most boys his age in that part of the country.

In 1859, when he was sixteen years old, young Theophilus entered Mossey Creek Baptist College in Jefferson County near his birthplace. Mossey Creek was a "scientific, literary and theological institution," whose president was N.B. Goforth. The members of the faculty were all religious, and many of the students were young men preparing for the ministry. Under such influence, young Theophilus became interested in the subject of religion, and when a revival meeting was started, he was among the first who put themselves forward to "seek religion." Though he was typically zealous in his efforts to "get religion," he did not succeed. He was greatly distressed because he could not "get religion," and yet, as he later observed, his experience during that revival was his best preparation for the ministry.[9] Although he considered himself a failure with respect to "getting religion," he resolved to pray regularly, read the Bible every day, and do everything the Book required.

Meanwhile, back at home, another influence had come to bear on his family. A gospel preacher by the name of Madison Love from North Alabama had traveled through Sequatchie Valley preaching. Larimore's mother and sister had obeyed the gospel after hearing him preach. When young Theophilus returned home from school, his mother said, "My son, your sister and I have been baptized." He replied, "When did you get religion?" His mother answered, "You don't have to get religion, you practice it." She then told him some things he had never heard about the gospel plan of salvation.[10]

The life of the family was disrupted for a time by the war. Just after completing his course of study at Mossey Creek and bringing home a diploma and a record as one of the school's best students, Theophilus enlisted in the Confederate Army. As would be expected of a man of his character, he served as a faithful and courageous soldier. While stationed at Chattanooga, he was captured when on a scouting expedition and sent to Federal headquarters. There he was offered a choice between taking "the non-combatant oath" or going to prison. He took the oath and returned home. A half-brother, Cassander Parendo Adolpheus, had entered the war at the age of sixteen and was never heard from again.

Near the close of the war Theophilus moved his mother and sisters in a wagon from East Tennessee into Kentucky, settling near Hopkinsville. They were without food in a strange land, with no means of support but his own labor and the wagon and team which they owned, Theophilus managed to make a meager living by cutting and hauling wood. He bore the responsibilities of a much older man.

Their religious life took more favorable turns. His mother was a Christian, and she straightway made herself known to the congregation in Hopkinsville. By and by Theophilus began to attend the meetings of the church with his mother and sisters. Soon he decided to become a Christian and spend the remainder of his life in service to the Lord. On his twenty-first birthday— July 10, 1864—he obeyed the gospel at a meeting of the church in Hopkinsville. As no regular preacher was present, B.S. Campbell, one of the elders, took his confession, after which E.H. Hopper, another one of the elders, baptized him.

He began to preach almost immediately after his baptism. He took as the text of his first sermon Luke 12:20, 21. Years later, commenting on that sermon, he wrote:

> My preaching began in Hopkinsville, Kentucky, in the meetinghouse in which I made the good confession....One thing about my sermon, if indeed it be lawful to call it a sermon, may be worthy of note, and that is, I wrote it. Having written it, I memorized it, and having memorized it, I repeated it over and over again in the presence of the team with which I was hauling wood in town, before I preached it to the people who patiently and politely listened to it.[11]

At the close of that first sermon, Miss Editha Retter, whose father was a member of Congress, made the good confession. This was a great source of encouragement to the young preacher. From the beginning, he attracted attention as a persuasive speaker and consecrated Christian.

Though he continued to preach, Larimore welcomed the opportunity to teach. He taught for a while at the Hopkinsville Female Institute under the superintendency of Enos Campbell and J.C. Campbell; when he decided to leave, it was with a splendid recommendation, which follows:

> Hopkinsville, KY.
> August 5, 1864
> We the undersigned take pleasure in recommending T.B. Larimore, as a teacher in any school, embracing such studies as Reading, Writing, Arithmetic, Grammar, Geography, Philosophy, Astronomy, etc., also in primary Algebra and Geometry, and we believe he will be faithful in the performance of his duties as head of a school (having this day examined him).
> Enos Campbell
> J. C. Campbell [12]

Encouraged as he was by his early success in teaching, Larimore at this time was convinced of his need for more formal training. Consequently, in the fall of 1866, he entered Franklin College near Nashville, Tennessee. This was the last school he attended, and he made a fine record, graduating with honors in 1867 or 1868 as valedictorian of his class.

A lasting influence upon his life was wrought by Tolbert Fanning, president of Franklin College, said to have been "both physically and intellectually, a giant."[13] Concerning President Fanning, Larimore wrote:

> He was a logician, an orator, and a judge of human nature—a marvelous judge of men and things. While I have neither right nor inclination to speak disparagingly of any brother, any preacher, any person, I deem it perfectly proper, because—strictly true, to say, Tolbert Fanning was, in some respects, a preacher without a peer....He evidently believed, without distressing, disturbing doubt or mental reservations, the gospel to be 'the power of God unto salvation'; and he never tired of preaching it, in its peerless, primitive purity, and sweet, sublime simplicity, without much variety or phraseology, but with a power and pathos that carried conviction to the hearts of those who diligently heard him.[14]

Larimore was greatly influenced by the teaching of Fanning. About thirty-five years after he was a student at Franklin College, he wrote:

Tolbert Fanning taught me to—like Paul, the peerless apostle—"never make merchandise of the gospel—never preach for pay." He said: "Christians, properly taught, will always liberally support any preacher worthy of such support"...."Trust the Lord and do your duty, and Providence will provide for you. The Lord's people will take care of you. When Christians, properly taught, cease to support a preacher—cease to thus and otherwise encourage him to preach—he should accept that as unmistakable evidence that his day of usefulness has passed, and quit."[15]

Larimore never ceased to cherish the words Fanning said to him when he left Franklin College as a young graduate:

The sages who had trimmed and taught me there handed me as complimentary a letter of commendation, as Christian, teacher and scholar, as any youth has ever received, I presume. Indeed, it could scarcely have been made stronger or more complimentary. When we said good-by, "Ol Boss," as many—never I—affectionately called him—Tolbert Fanning—said to me: "I have never failed to correctly read a man when I had a good chance. You may never accumulate a fortune, but you'll never depart from the faith or bring reproach upon the cause of Christ."[16]

On June 2, 1867, Larimore preached at Burnett's Chapel in Davidson County, Tennessee. At the conclusion of the sermon, C. G. Payton of Hart County, Kentucky—a former classmate at Franklin College—came forward and made the good confession. By request of Payton, they went together to Green's Chapel, Hart County, Kentucky, where the baptism took place on June 16, 1867. This was the first person he baptized.[17] This was an event which stood out in his mind, as did the first funeral service, which was at the burial of "sister Sinclair's little baby boy, age six weeks, near Thompson's Station, Tennessee." This event occurred on July 12, 1867.[18]

After leaving Franklin College, Larimore traveled with R. B. Trimble throughout Middle Tennessee. They preached in private homes, under trees, in school houses, at country churches—anywhere they could get a congregation to listen to them. They traveled on horseback. Trimble did most of the preaching. The experience of Trimble was needed to solidify the churches which had been disorganized by the war. Occasionally, however, when conditions were favorable, Larimore would preach. Trimble said that Larimore "was the

most devoted and self-forgetful young preacher he
ever knew."[19]

It was through the influence of Trimble that
Larimore went down into Alabama. At first he
taught at Mountain Home in Lawrence County,
where the brethren under the leadership of J. M.
Pickens were trying to establish a college. He
remained there until the summer of 1868, when he
went to preach in Franklin and Lauderdale
Counties during a school vacation period.

On August 30, 1868, he was married to Miss
Esther Gresham near Florence, Alabama. In the fall
of that year he resumed teaching at Mountain
Home. That enterprise failed, and at the beginning
of 1869 he went to teach at Mansell Kendrick's in
West Tennessee. He taught there for six months
and at Stantonville, Tennessee for ten months,
after which he returned to his home near Florence,
Alabama, known now throughout the brotherhood
as "Mars Hill."

Bolstered by the encouragement of his wife,
Esther, he was determined to establish a school for
boys and girls. This was a colossal undertaking for
two impoverished young people, but they were
"brave, hopeful, self-reliant, resourceful, energetic,
and industrious."[20] He borrowed money with
which to erect the necessary buildings for the
school and helped to do the work—"handled lum-
ber, shoveled dirt, made mortar, sawed timber, carried brick, hauled shingles, chopped logs and

cheered the workmen."[21] Mars Hill College opened the first day of 1871 and continued to 1887. The school was patronized by the brotherhood and others throughout the Southern states. Among the prominent preachers who attended the school were F. C. Sowell, E. A. Elam, F. D. And F. B. Srygley, Lee Jackson, J. C. McQuiddy, and a host of others.

During the existence of the school, seven children were born to the Larimores: Mary Delilah or "Dedie," as she was lovingly called; Granville Lipscomb; Theophilus Brown, called "Toppie"; William Herschell, known as "Herschell"; Julia Esther, called "Ettie"; Andrew Virgil, or "Virgil"; and a baby girl, Minnie Bell, who died shortly after birth.

F. D. Srygley, who was Larimore's closest friend, wrote:

> Mars Hill College never failed, but was abandoned because a wider field of usefulness opened before its president....More than once I have seen him (Larimore) shed tears over piles of letters begging for preaching when he was confined by college duties at Mars Hill. He would say he had no heart to be there teaching children English grammar when a perishing world was pleading with him to tell them of Jesus and his love. Those of us who knew his feelings and understood the situation advised the suspension of the college. After more than seven

years' steady persuasion on our part, and serious, prayerful consideration on his part, the school was abandoned.[22]

So Larimore turned his back upon a place and an enterprise that he loved; and he turned his face toward a pleading, needing world. The stage was set for his entrance as an evangelist without a peer—and a preacher whose reaching, yearning heart saw no equal.

CHAPTER III

# MATURE YEARS:
# FAMILY TIES

T. B. Larimore was forty-four years old when Mars Hill College was closed. When he reluctantly left his beloved Mars Hill home, he "went everywhere preaching the word"—traveling from "Maine to Mexico, from the Carolinas to California"—often staying away from home for months at a time, always busy, always receiving more calls than he could accept, hurrying from one appointment to another. His program for preaching was "twice every day and three times every Sunday." At his back he must always have been aware of "time's winged chariot," for, he said, "The wide, wide world is my field."

While Larimore traversed the "wide, wide world" preaching the gospel, his family remained at home, working on the farm and doing whatever was necessary to hold the family together. Though they must have sorely missed the beloved husband and father, they learned to cope with his absence. A letter dated September 2, 1894, includes a revealing observation from Dedie to her grandmother Larimore. She wrote that "Papa slipped in on us last night" after an absence of several weeks. She told how he was going to preach "twice a day and three times on Sunday" at the church in Florence. She also mentioned that the boys were busy harvesting the crops and that the girls had helped their mother put up a "barrel of kraut, fourteen quarts of tomatoes, and forty gallons of apples." She proceeded to share with her grandmother other items of interest. They were all proud that Herschell's colt had won a blue ribbon at the colt show in Florence. She expressed relief that Toppie was feeling better after a painful spell with his leg. She said that a girl had been hired to help them with their chores for the sum of two dollars and fifty cents per month.[1]

So life went on at home, and Larimore was able, with some peace of mind, to grasp every opportunity to preach the word. The entire Larimore family was united in sacrificial love for another, with emphasis on their love for the Lord.

Obviously, if one lives very long in this world, he comes to the Garden of Gethsemane, the place of sorrow. Larimore was no exception. He was well acquainted with sorrow. His mother, to whom he was devoted, left the scenes of this earth on a bright September day in 1902. She was in her ninetieth year. Writing about his mother, Larimore said:

> She devoted about half of her days to the service of the Lord: nearly all of them to the service of humanity. Always poor in a financial sense, she was 'rich in faith'—living faith—and had right to rejoice when she read, in the love language of the Book of books, 'Hearken, my beloved brethren, hath not God chosen the poor of this world rich in faith, and heirs of the kingdom which he hath promised to them that love him?'...To her children, she left a priceless heritage: the memory of a true, tender-hearted mother who loved and served the Lord. It was their will, as well as hers, that she should give all she had to give, save her love and her prayers for them, to others—which she did. Then she and they were satisfied, and loved each other all the more tenderly.[2]

Larimore had a tender love for his mother that is seldom matched in this world of coldness, selfishness, and indifference. His love for her had an early beginning, and it grew stronger throughout the years.

One remembered incident exemplifies the early ties of parent and child; and it gives one understanding of the mutual affection and loyalty. When he was but a small boy, he accompanied his mother to the home of a neighbor with whom they were to spend the night. In the barnyard there was a flock of geese with which young Theophilos was greatly pleased. Some young ladies playfully told him that if he would catch one, they would have it for supper. Having no idea that the tyke could catch the goose, they soon dismissed the whole matter from their minds. After a while, to their great astonishment, he came to the house, packing a struggling goose in his arms. He handed it over to the young ladies, who shortly released it and gave it not another thought until the family and their guests gathered around the supper table. As they sat at the table, Theophilos was asked what he would have to eat. He replied, "If you please, ma'am, I will have some of the goose." He was told that the goose was not cooked. He replied by saying that he would wait until they cooked the goose. When he was told that it was too late to cook the goose, he firmly answered, "If there ain't no goose, I don't want no supper."[3] He had set his heart on that goose for supper, and, while he was not ugly about the matter, he did not for the moment think of anything else he cared to eat.

This little incident remained vivid in the memory of Theophilos Larimore, and it also touched his mother's heart forever. So when her beloved son announced his determination to leave home to attend college, she thought of that disappointing occasion when her son looked in vain for goose upon the table before him. She resolved to give him a surprise to equal and soften that childhood disappointment. Without letting him know what she was planning, she procured a young goose. She secretly prepared it for his lunch on the road the day he was to leave home for college. It must have been with mixed feelings of excitement and loss that she packed a lunch basket with all the good things that he liked to eat—and the goose, juicy and fragrant. Finally, she put the lunch basket into his hand and kissed him a loving good-bye.

He turned his back upon mother and home and walked steadily all morning. About noon, he reached the brow of Cumberland Mountain overlooking the beautiful valley below. A few minutes of brisk walking down the mountainside brought him to a beautiful spring beside the road. Here he stopped, weary, hungry, footsore—and painfully homesick. But when he opened the little basket, the fountain of tears broke loose, and he wept unashamedly, like a small child. He knew that what his mother had prepared for him was far and away better than anything she had for herself. He was so completely overcome by his emotions that he found it impossible to eat a bite. He tenderly closed the basket and gave himself to serious meditation until, glancing at the sun, he realized that he must move on if he was to reach his destination before nightfall.[4] Years later, thinking of this incident, he wrote:

> The mountain was between me and my mother. The valley was spread before me in beauty that beggars description. The river, like a silver thread of life, wound its course through the valley below me. Before me was college with all its ambition; but behind me was mother in her loneliness, dearer to my heart than all else beside. As I pondered and wept, I almost resolved to retrace my steps, give up my aspirations and die in obscurity by my mother's side. Nothing but the knowledge that it was her desire for me to go to college and that she would be displeased if I returned to her, caused me to decide to go on. So taking up my precious basket I continued my journey down the mountain, finishing the walk of forty miles by night without eating a mouthful of anything.[5]

The tie between brother Larimore and his mother was so strong, so close, so tender, that as long as he lived he mentioned her with great affection.

On August 4, 1903, death once again took its toll from the Larimore household. This time it was Theophilos Brown Larimore, Jr.—"Toppie," as he was called—who went the way of all flesh. Toppie was thirty-one years of age.

His had been a life of suffering but, even more, of great courage and fortitude. When he was about seventeen years old, he injured his hip while riding a horse. He was confined to his bed for several months. Though he was given the best of care, his condition continued to worsen. The injury to his hip was permanent. He never again walked without crutches, but he bore his misfortune with cheerfulness, thus further endearing himself to his family. After a year of suffering, he began to show some improvement. He attended Florence Normal College and began to prepare for the profession of Osteopathy. He graduated at Kirksville, Missouri; in February 1900, he located in Winchester, Tennessee, and began the practice of his profession. As the months and years went by, however, Toppie's condition continued to worsen, until he was forced to leave his profession and return home to Mars Hill. He was taken shortly afterward to a Nashville hospital for surgery. In spite of the top medical attention he received, he passed away. It was August 1903. His death brought unspeakable sadness to every member of the Larimore family. Herschell, who was unable to attend the funeral, wrote his mother as follows:

I am so crushed and broken-hearted I don't know what to say to you, to lighten your load of grief. You have lost your best boy, the one you loved best, I know, because he was the most lovable.[6]

Five days after Toppie passed away—three days after his burial, the annual meeting at Mars Hill began. It was a sad meeting for the Mars Hill family—especially for the father and mother, who missed the bright face of their son. How could they go on without the one who had never failed to be with them at their reunion time, always happy and cheerful, always doing everything in his power to add to the happiness of others by many simple little things that no one else would think of doing?[7]

With Spartan courage, Larimore opened the meeting, using as his text I Peter 3:15. He looked to the sure source of comfort to which he had directed so many sorrowing souls. He found grace to bear the trial, and he preached the Word with deeper pathos and power because of the sorrow that filled and crushed and overwhelmed his own heart.

At the time of Toppie's passing away, his mother was in poor health, and it was feared that she would not survive the shock of his sudden passing. However, she bore her grief with Christian fortitude. The time was all too short, though, until Larimore had to endure the loss of his mate as well. He wrote of her:

> She is patient as patience itself. I've managed to be cheerful—appear so, at least—ever since I came home until today. When I broke down this morning, she said: "You oughtn't to grieve to give me up. My life has been a life of sorrow, of suffering, for three years—four years next August." That means ever since "Toppie" went away. His final farewell, "Good-bye, mama," will linger in her heart while she lingers here.[8]

Her family gave her loving attention as her life waned. Her eldest son, Granville, whose home was in Tampa, Florida, could be with her but little. But Herschell and Dedie were devoted and constant nurses. A year before her passing, Larimore gave up his heavy schedule of evangelistic work and went home to nurse his companion—the beloved mother of Mars Hill. She protested against his giving up his work, saying, "I don't think it's right to keep you from doing what duty demands"; but he replied, "Duty demands but one thing now, and that is to nurse you."[9] He left her bedside no more except at her urgent request, when she realized the need for his service in some specially loved place in his field of work.

She gave directions for her funeral as quietly as she had been accustomed to give directions about household affairs. On the morning of March 4, 1907, the long, brave battle for life ended, and the patient sufferer passed into peace eternal. The next day, her body was robed, as she had requested, in her wedding dress, which she had carefully kept so long for that sad departure. She was laid to rest in the burying ground of the Gresham family, close to the house in which she was born.

In the *Gospel Advocate* of July 18, 1907, under the caption "Julia Esther Gresham Larimore," Emma Page wrote a lengthy article on the life and death of Mrs. Larimore.[10] Miss Page said in part:

> She was indeed a help meet for her husband. Her practical business knowledge, industry, economy and unfailing cheerfulness were invaluable to him in his work as teacher and evangelist....They were rich in hope, love for each other and for the cause of Christ, as well as sympathy for suffering humanity...It may truly be said of her: "Her children rise up and call her blessed." By reason of brother Larimore's absence from home, much of the training of their children devolved upon her; and she did that work wisely and well. She lived to see all of them

grown to manhood and womanhood, all faithful, loyal Christians, living busy, useful lives.[11]

The three Mars Hill "boys" she selected to conduct her funeral services were R. P. Meeks, J. C. McQuiddy, and E. A. Elam.[12]

On her tombstone, Larimore had the following words engraved:

> A dutiful daughter; an affectionate sister; a faithful friend; a loyal, helpful, hopeful wife; a model mother; a sweet singer; a truly conscientious, consistent Christian, always consecrated, loyal and true to Christ and his cause, she was perfectly prepared for that sweet home where sorrows and sad separations are unknown—"where life is eternal and a treasure sublime." "Farewell, sweet wife—by grace divine, We'll meet you 'over there.'"

Your Lonely Husband[13]

## CHAPTER IV

# MARVELOUS MEETINGS

A trip to Mars Hill may take one to that meetinghouse and the creek where Larimore baptized hundreds of people during his famous meetings there. The creek is no longer used, thanks to the installation of a baptistery; but surely there are echoes of those melodious tones—and whispers of love and gratitude and joy such as touched the hearts and lives of so many.

The central thought of Larimore's preaching was "Christ and him Crucified." But his preaching involved every facet of the "sweet, sad story" of Jesus and his redeeming love. Some of the sermon topics that he used reflect his adherence to the basic theme: "The Great Commission"; "The

Glorious Gospel of Christ"; "Fellowship"; "The Lord's Supper"; "The Army of the Lord"; "Be Ye All of One Mind"; "The Whole Duty of Man"; "Rest for the Soul"; "Christ and Christians"; "The Iron, the Silver, and the Golden Rule"; "The Prayer of the Cross"; Existence and Value of the Soul." Often he would preach a week or more on one text such as Matthew 16:18 and Hebrews 11:6. To "preach the word" was his commitment.

A young preacher wrote him to ask, "What kind of preaching is most needed in a protracted meeting?" He replied:

What kind of preaching is most needed in a protracted meeting? Gospel preaching....Paul's kind of preaching—not "another gospel"—is the kind needed and we must avoid all other....Study, work and pray, always doing your best. No gospel preacher should ever be satisfied to do less than his best—no one, of course, can do more. Of course, the purest, wisest and best preachers may have their hobbies, opinions, personal preferences, and possibly, even prejudices; but the word of the Lord ever, and these never, should be preached. Sinners should be taught how to become Christians; Christians should be taught how to make their calling and election sure; and all should be earnestly, tenderly and lovingly exhorted to abandon all evil, 'abstain from all appearance of evil,' and walk in the light of God's eternal truth.[1]

His success as a preacher was phenomenal. This success was due, not only to his natural ability, including his rare gifts as a speaker; but it may be traced in large measure to hard and diligent work. He had a regular, constant, systematic program of study. These firm rules guided him in sermon preparation:

Always study, to know what to say and how to say it. Leave nothing to chance.

Study. Always do your best. Always notice everything carefully before beginning the discourse—fire, light, ventilation—everything—and then neither notice nor know anything but your own business till the close of that meeting.[2]

Concerning the source from which he drew material for his sermons, he said:

My shot and shell are not manufactured by man. My gun is always loaded, and is fired automatically. My ammunition comes from the Arsenal above, while I draw from memory's store as apt illustrations as I can, and try, as did our Savior, to simplify my teaching by illustration and analogy. I rely always, for proof, on God's eternal truth alone.[3]

After hearing Larimore preach at Whitewright, Texas, Thomas E. Milholland wrote:

He is a wonderful preacher—inexhaustible in resources; rich in thought, abounding in imagery; clear and convincing in argument; plain but powerful in delivery.[4]

As a preacher of "the Word" he was free from sensational methods, low slang, and vulgar catch-phrases. He never sought to popularize his sermons by using wit or humor. He never resorted to frivolous anecdotes to illustrate an argument or catch the attention of an audience. His was a solemn and earnest presentation of the gospel.

As a polished scholar and an accomplished rhetorician, he was an expert in the use of the English language. Everyone who heard him was "charmed by the accuracy and nice discrimination" he manifested in the use of his native tongue. Through the selection of words, the formation of sentences, and distinct enunciation of each word in a sentence, every syllable in a word, and even each letter in the syllable, his delivery had for his listeners a fascination like that of music. Every sermon he preached bore eloquent testimony to his perfect familiarity with the common version of the Bible. He not only read the Bible much, but he also studied it carefully, sentence by sentence, word by word. Those sermons which have been preserved are replete with Bible information, and they are unfailingly expressed in faultless English. Like Paul, he relied upon the revelation of God, rather than the wisdom of man, in his preaching.

The power of his delivery stood in contrast to his understated personality. He was reticent, emotionally non-combative, and thoroughly devotional by nature. His appearance often displayed a deep sadness, which was no doubt due to the fact that he regarded the preaching of the gospel as a very serious business indeed.

F. D. Srygley pointed out that Larimore's emotional nature was variable in its moods.

He was either on the mountain of transfiguration or leaning over the bridge of sighs. One day he gushes with David, "Bless the Lord, oh my soul, and all that is within me bless his holy name"; the next, he laments with Paul, "If in this life only we have hope in Christ we are of all men most miserable." It is difficult to determine which of those moods is the most favorable for effective speaking with him. When he speaks from the top of the mountain his sermons encourage, elevate, inspire and electrify an audience; when he preaches from the bridge of sighs his hearers are subdued, deeply moved with sympathy, impressed with the worthlessness of this world and its joys and sobered down to a deeper piety and a firmer faith. He never stirs up strife nor provokes antagonism. He is not combative in nature, and his sermons never arouse a war-like feeling where he goes. He is a religious man by nature, and pious by life-long training. He lives near to his God every hour in his faith and feeling....His power in the pulpit consists mainly in the plainness with which he states his proposition, and the pathos and persuasiveness with which he appeals to the hearts of the people in exhortation. The intellect readily approves the correctness of his doctrine, and the heart warmly responds to the tenderness of his appeal.[5]

Here was a man who, at all times, was unassuming, frank, dignified, and courteous. Yet when he spoke, he captured hearts and minds and confidence. Srygley said:

His voice was the wonder and delight of all who heard him. It was strong and sonorous, but well modulated and full of tenderness, love and persuasive pathos, that gave a new beauty and power to the plain commandments of God and the touching story of the cross. In exhortation, he melted an audience to tears as if by magic, and the love of God, the death of Christ and the hope of the saints were the only themes he chose during all that meeting for the exhortations that followed every sermon with such good effects.[6]

Regardless of his natural and acquired abilities, this great speaker in no way wanted to call attention to himself or to any element of his sermon for the sake of shallow display or cheap showmanship. In writing to a young man who was just beginning to preach, he said:

Rely on the truth ever: on bare assertion, never. Prove the points you preach. Let your preaching abound in appropriate illustrations, and make it plain enough for the comprehension of little children, if you can. Thus the Savior taught, and his way is always best. Avoid bragging, boasting, and ostentation. Say little—very little—about yourself; and when you do talk about yourself, say "I" "me," or "mine,"—never "we," "us," or "our." Bad grammar is no evidence of lack of egotism. I know a preacher who is evidently about as full of egotism as an eggshell, in its normal condition, is of egg, who refers to himself as "we," "us," and "our," probably forty times in forty minutes, in his preaching sometimes. There is just as much egotism in "fiddlesticks" as in "I," meaning "I"; and the same is true of every substitute for "I," including that much used, much abused expression so often met with in preachers' reports, "the writer." The use of "I" certainly does not show more egotism than to use "the writer," since there is at least a strong implication in the use of the latter that the user has a monopoly on the business of writing. When you mean "I," say "I." That's the sensible thing to do.[7]

Batsell Barrett Baxter gives this appraisal of the preaching of Larimore:

First, what was the secret of his power? T. B. Larimore was unusually blessed with a rich melodious voice and an appealing personal appearance. Immediately, people liked him when they first saw and heard him. His voice commanded respect, conveyed his meanings clearly and pleasantly, and generally made a fine impression upon his hearers. His preaching and manner were such as to appeal to people also. There was a kindness, an evident warmth of personal concern for his hearers, and a friendliness that made him unusually effective. No preacher of his generation got closer to the hearts of those who heard him than did T. B. Larimore.[8]

In a letter to one of his boys on "how to preach," he said: "The way to preach is to preach. Just get full of spirit and truth and turn yourself loose. As a good old brother once expressed it, 'Just fill the barrell full, knock the bung out, and let 'er come. That's the way to preach.'"

The eloquence of Larimore was proverbial. C.E.W. Dorris voices his impression of his preaching after first hearing him:

> In 1893, he held a meeting in Nashville. It was my second year in the Nashville Bible School. I had heard so much about his fine oratory that I expected him to stay among the moon and stars. He preached on the New Birth. He never took a single flight. He fell so far short of what I expected to hear that it took me two weeks to get up enough courage to hear him again. I did not expect to hear much, but he came between my two extremes and redeemed himself. After that I appreciated his preaching.[9]

Larimore, even as a young man, aspired to be an orator. He confessed, "I always felt like I wanted to be an orator."[10] He would slip out into the woods alone, stand up with as much dignity as a senator, repeat meaningless sentences, and imagine himself addressing a vast concourse of people.

Frank Boyd, a prominent lawyer and former Mars Hill student, wrote of an incident in school which vividly portrays the rich eloquence of Larimore. It was the custom of Professor Larimore to lecture each Saturday morning from eleven to noon. On this particular day he chose as his subject the life of Napoleon Bonaparte. He gave a masterly review of the life of the "Little Corporal," who had a burning ambition to place himself at the head of an empire embracing all Europe, but who, instead, died in exile. In contrast with Napoleon's career, he drew a word picture of an earnest Christian life, with its measureless influences for good.

Dinner time came; but he was in the midst of a tide of eloquence and pathos so earnest, so powerful, that there was no stopping: no one thought of the lapse of time. The students sat, silent, paying him the voluntary tribute of almost breathless attention; and when, after another hour had passed, he closed that wonderful speech, many were weeping; others, with pale faces, seemed as if awaking from a dream; and one little girl rushed to brother Larimore and sobbed in his arms. He soothed the child

with a tender caress, and, with a few quiet
words, dismissed the students bringing
them down gently from the height to which
his eloquence had borne them.[11]

The eloquence of Larimore is graphically
described in a clipping from the Madisonville (Ky.)
Mail, quoted Srygley:

T. B. Larimore has been with us, to
"preach the word" to build us up, to make us
one, to make us better, to make us happier,
to strengthen saints, to save souls, and has
gone to other fields to sow seeds of righteousness, unity, peace and love...I have heard
Governor Bob Taylor in his happiest moods,
and have followed him in his loftiest flights
of fancy and dream. I have heard him on "The
Fiddle and the Bow," when he touched every
chord in the soul that can be touched by all
that is pathetic and tender and sweet, and
soul-inspiring. I have heard him on "Paradise
of Fools," as he talked thrillingly of "God's
first thought for the happiness of man," and
he filled my heart with gentleness, kindness
and love—sweetest sentiments of the soul: I
have heard him on "Visions and Dreams,"
when he so eloquently and tenderly told of
his return to the dear old home of the "long,
long ago"; and he filled my mind with sweet,

sad memories of the delightful days, forever
gone, when I dwelt with father, mother, sisters, and brothers in the dear old home that
can never be home again. I have heard
Ditzler on "The Judgment Day," and he held
me fixed to my seat and overwhelmed with
horror as he depicted the tortures of tor-
ment and told of the shrieks of the doomed
banished into outer darkness forever
because of sin. I have heard him deliver his
"Hallelujah Sermon," and he pictured so
beautifully and vividly the beauty and
grandeur and glory of heaven that the flame
of love and reverence for heaven and heaven-
ly things he kindled in my breast has never
been extinguished, though long, eventful
years have come and gone since last I heard
him speak. (These are but some samples of
men and things I have heard and seen; yet, as
I sat, last Sunday, and listened to T.B.
Larimore as he reasoned of the "vanity of
vanities" in wisdom, wealth, pleasure,
power, and the alluring beauties of nature—
beautiful words of wisdom pouring in tor-
rents and bursting like flames from his lips,
and sparkling and scintillating as purest
gems of reason in brightest light of thought,
filling and flooding every mind present with
light almost divine—I voluntarily said,
"never man spake like this man"; and this

was the unanimous verdict of one of the largest and most intelligent audiences ever assembled in the city of Madisonville.)[12]

A sample of his eloquence is given in a sermon, "The Rock," No. 4:

Kingdoms may be founded, may flourish and may fall, but the church of Christ can never fall, can never fail. Atheism may assail, infidelity may sneer, skepticism may smile, and anxious hearts may fear for the safety of Zion, but Zion stands secure, backed by the promise of the great I Am that it shall never be destroyed, the literal, living, abiding fulfillment of the promise of the Lord Jesus Christ: "Upon this rock I will build my church and the gates of hades shall not prevail against it." The sun may be blotted out, the moon cease to reflect light, the stars may fall from the withering vault of night, and the heavens be rolled up like a scroll, the wreck of matter and the crash of worlds may come and the judgment day be set; but, when the angel of the Lord shall descend on pinions dipped in the lovelight enveloping the throne of God, and, planting one foot upon the land and one upon the sea, shall declare by Him who plants his footsteps upon the sea, and rides up on the

storm, that time was, time is, but time shall
be no more—even then the church of Christ
shall stand, secure as the throne of God
itself: for our Savior promised long ago, "the
gates of hell shall not prevail against it." And
Jehovah hath declared, "it shall never be
destroyed"; and the Holy Spirit by the pen of
Isaiah, the prophet, says: "The word of our
God shall stand forever."[13]

In 1888, after much urging, he consented to
conduct a meeting in Louisville, Kentucky. He had
never before preached so far north, and here for the
first time his preaching was subject to comparison
with that of some of the ablest men of the restoration. These were men whose sermons had never
reached the borders of his former fields of labor.
Louisville audiences were no strangers to Hopson,
Lard, Errett, and Campbell; and they were
acquainted with many others of equal merit as
determined by their pulpit ability. It was with con-
siderable misgiving, therefore, that he consented to
try to preach in Louisville at all. However, he fully
sustained his high reputation and more than lived
up to the expectations of those who had never
before heard his preaching. Some began by compar-
ing him to Hopson, then to Lard, and finally to Clay
as an orator; others readily and enthusiastically
pronounced him far superior to all of the rest.[14]

A unique Larimorean language enhanced the eloquence of the noted preacher. He made wide use of alliteration in his speaking as well as in his writing. In his preaching, he proposed "publicly, privately, and practically" to "preach and practice union and unity at all times." In a personal letter he wrote of "the bright blaze by night of brilliant, artistic electric lights that look like brilliant buds from the burning bush and blazing blossoms from the bosom of the sun."[15]

In a sermon on "The Rock" No. I, speaking of Peter's confession, Larimore said:

> It was in the coasts or immediate presence of this rock-founded, rock-builded, rock-bounded, rock-surrounded, rock-protected, rock-shadowed city that Jesus, the Rock of Ages, the Rock for sinners cleft, said to Peter, the "rock"—Cephos, the "stone"—in reference to that spiritual institution that had been represented by Daniel, in the then long ago, as a little rock cut out of the mountain without hands and subsequently filling the earth; that spiritual institution every member of which is called in the Bible a "lively stone" or a "living stone"; "Upon this rock I will build my church."[26]

Another example of his eloquent use of the English language is seen in a letter he wrote from Los Angeles, California, January 10, 1895:

Here I am, far away from home and friends and loved ones, farther than ever I've been before, in the "city of angels," hear the deep, deep sea, the ocean of oceans, the peerless Pacific, in a land of perennial verdure, a land of perpetual spring—grass growing, buds bursting, flowers blooming, fruits pending, vegetables maturing, sun shining, birds singing, and balmy breezes softly sighing all around me; while spotless snows that shroud the high hills defy the sun that strives in vain to give life and birth and being to vegetation on mountain heights above me.[17]

Sometimes he would speak of "the heavens bending in blue beauty above us," or "our guide through grace to glory and to God."[18] Whenever he engaged in a protracted meeting, his alliterations, rhetorical expressions, exquisite phrases, and chaste language were the "talk of the town." It is said that in his later years he studiously avoided flights of oratory because he was afraid the people might become more interested in his eloquence than in the preaching of the gospel. But it was impossible for Larimore to avoid eloquence in his speaking. It was just as natural with him as breathing. Eloquence flowed from his lips with rhythmic beauty. A commonplace announcement, when made by Larimore, was "a thing of beauty.

Not to exaggerate, the entire brotherhood was praising T. B. Larimore. Demands upon his time were tremendous. Soon after he recovered from a long spell of sickness, he wrote to Srygley:

> You can imagine—only imagine—how sorely I am perplexed, how I am worried. At least twenty places are pressing me to come, so that it truly grieves me to postpone going to any one of them, even for one day. Now, knowing me as you alone know me, consider the pressure from one source, and then multiply that by twenty, and you can imagine how I am distressed. I have not kept count of calls this year, but I believe I have been urged to go to one thousand different places. What to do I know not. Well, I'll continue to try to do all that duty demands.[19]

It was not just to pulpits in far-flung places that he was called. He was deluged with offers to become president of various colleges as well as minister of large and influential churches. The brethren in Cookeville, Tennessee, wanted him to become chancellor of "Larimore University," which they desired to build. In 1911, J.M. McCaleb, a missionary in Japan, suggested that Larimore make a world preaching tour. Larimore replied, "...if duty demands; the Lord calls; and if our friends wish to send me, I know no reason why I should not go."[20] It seems almost impossible to comprehend any man receiving as much praise as was heaped upon Larimore without becoming egotistical. He constantly received letters filled with expressions of love, tenderness, admiration, and praise. So what was the shield which protected him from vanity and egotism? Possibly a partial answer is found in the clouds that had hung over Larimore's childhood and youth. They wrought a salutary effect upon his character in other respects, perhaps in this area as well. Praise that might have been dangerous or ruinous to a less well-balanced man seemed never to disturb the serenity of his calm, thoughtful mind; his patient, meek humility; his frank natural manner; his perfect balance of thought and feeling. He appreciated the love and praise so abundantly showered upon him, but there was never in his mind any hint of a "holier-than-thou" attitude.

As a matter of fact, warmed as he was, encouraged as he must have been by these accolades, Larimore realized perfectly well the perils that lurked in overmuch praise.

Larimore was convinced of the efficacy of sustained meetings. His longest meeting, held in Sherman, Texas, began on January 4, 1894, and continued for twenty-two weeks and one day. During that meeting, he preached three hundred and thirty-three sermons, and there were about three hundred additions. What strength and effort were demanded of him could not be imagined. But he believed so strongly in the potential for good that he was more than willing to make the necessary investment of himself.

Larimore conducted several other long meetings in various parts of the country. Always, day after day, week after week, he faced an expectant audience at the scheduled time. Promptness was almost a hobby with him. He was especially careful to begin every service at exactly the hour—the very moment—announced for that service. Commenting on this matter, Larimore said: "When I say, the Lord willing, our service will begin at seven o'clock, those who know me are sure they will begin just sixty minutes after six—and they do, too."

As he faced an audience to preach twice each day and three times on Sunday, there was nothing in his appearance or delivery which was intended to distract or to belittle the power of the Word. He was always simply attired. He never wore a tie. He wore a sort of "clerical" collar. He never stood behind a pulpit or lectern of any kind. It was his custom to read a chapter from the Bible, then repeat it from memory and proceed with his sermon without making use of manuscript or notes. He stood erect—seldom moving after the beginning of the sermon. His gestures were rare. He depended on "the Word" and the Word only to attract and hold the people. In nearly every sermon he would quote or refer to the Great Commission. He looked upon this passage as basic to preaching the Gospel.

For many years, Larimore thought of himself as a "country preacher," preferring to make his appeals in rural communities. His great success with rural audiences had attracted attention throughout the South, and his labors had often been earnestly solicited in many important cities; but with few exceptions, he had declined all such invitations. It was simply his preference to preach in the country; furthermore, he had a feeling that he could never succeed as a "city preacher."

In spite of his reluctance, he was willing to preach in cities if he became convinced that he would best serve the Lord in an urban setting. Still, he continued to turn down the numerous calls from city churches until 1885. After what turned into years of prayerful deliberation, he decided to make two important changes—holding longer meetings and preaching in cities. This was in the fall of 1885.

He was not yet totally convinced of taking this new direction. R. L. Cave, a preacher from Nashville, made a long, tedious trip to a country church where Larimore was holding a meeting. He arrived on horseback from the railroad, determined to appeal in person for Larimore to come to Nashville to hold a meeting.

Finally he promised to go; but immediately he began to regret his promise. He feared failure. At that particular time, Nashville was wild with admiration for Sam Jones' style of preaching. It would have been difficult, indeed, to find a man nearer to Jones' opposite than T. B. Larimore. The latter never told frivolous anecdotes in the pulpit, never used a slang phrase or rough expression, never approximated anything sensational or sought notoriety in anything remotely bordering upon levity.

The meeting with the Church Street church began in November and continued about thirty days, resulting in seventy-five additions to this congregation for which David Lipscomb served as an elder. In 1887 he held another meeting in Nashville, one which lasted for six weeks and resulted in one hundred and twenty-six baptisms. Larimore's decision regarding long meetings led to a number of notable engagements from coast to coast. In 1888 he conducted a month-long meeting in Fort Smith, Arkansas, with fifty baptisms. By that time invitations multiplied to a number which "would certainly aggregate to over 360 and probably to 500." In 1888, he also conducted a month's meeting in Louisville, resulting in seventy additions.

Other meetings of note spread the word of his success. In July 1870, he held a meeting in Collierville, Tennessee, with eighty-one additions. In Lauderdale County in the same year, a week's meeting resulted in fifty-two additions. In Pocahontas, Tennessee, in 1872, he held a seven-day meeting and baptized thirty-two people. M. H. Northcross, who became a noted preacher, was baptized during that meeting. In the same year he preached in a ten-day meeting in Greenwood, Tennessee, with sixty-one additions. In 1874, he delivered a series of sermons in Linden Street Christian church. There were twenty baptisms. In 1895, he held a meeting in Los Angeles, California, from January 3 to April 17, with one hundred and twenty-five baptisms resulting. On and on he went, from coast to coast, and from hungry group to yet another hungry group, "preaching the word" to vast audiences and baptizing thousands.

By special request, Larimore delivered an address before the Memphis and Shelby County Bible Society in the First Presbyterian Church of Memphis, Tennessee, Sunday evening, March 1, 1874, on "God and the Bible." Upon receiving a copy of this address, Mrs. Alexander Campbell wrote:

I am so glad to see, my dear brother, that you were entirely absorbed in the grandeur of your theme. I notice that the large "I" did not stand out once before you; but the great I Am occupied your wonder, admiration, gratitude and love. "God and the Bible" is the most exalted and loftiest theme that could engage the tongue of man or seraph. Your collation of truths in defense of the Bible and the God of the Bible can never be set aside or refuted by the strongest opposers, either Deistical or Atheistical, upon earth.[21]

While holding a meeting in Lexington, Kentucky, in 1889, Larimore wrote:

Our venerable, saintly sister, Mrs. Alexander Campbell, who has been on her journey from the cradle to the grave nearly ninety years, cheered the hearts of the faithful few who were bravely battling against wind and wave and weather, to hold the old ship steady through the storm, by her blessed, hopeful presence....Sister Campbell reached Lexington in a snowstorm that night, too late for supper, and reached our meetinghouse on time. She said, "We started early this morning, and have had no dinner today; but I must attend the meeting, and be on time, lest being late, I disturb someone; so I will postpone my supper till tomorrow morning"—which she did. Blessed be the memory and bright be the crown of all such souls.[22]

While Larimore was engaged in his long meeting of five months' duration at Sherman, Texas, in 1894, F. D. Srygley wrote him, asking about the progress of the meeting, its probable length—it had thus far been in progress for nine weeks—how the preacher could stand such long-continued work, and how and where he found material for sermons, etc. He received the following reply:

Yours received. Much obliged. I hastily answer the best I can. We are just now beginning to get things loosened up at the roots. The interest is increasing every day. You are anxious to know how I am holding up. I am well. Nothing can be better for me than to preach twice every day and three times on Sunday, unless it is to preach three times every day and Sunday too. My voice? It's all right. Length of sermons? Fifty minutes. Entire service: Seventy minutes. When is the meeting to close? No mortal knows. Subjects and materials for sermons? The Bible is full of them. Its treasures are simply inexhaustible. Study? That I do. I am not only studying, but learning—learning rapidly every day. I see new beauties in the Bible every day, and am astonished at the sweet, sublime simplicity of God's eternal truth. Exhaust Bible themes and thoughts and truths at this rate, after a while? Yes, when swallows drink the ocean dry. What books do I consult? The Bible, Webster's Dictionary and the Bible—these three, and no more. How long do I purpose to fight on this line? Till mustered out of service.[23]

For approximately forty years brother Larimore held a meeting at Mars Hill every August. It was a big event in that part of the country, one in which hundreds of his neighbors and friends assembled to hear the great man preach. Every year large numbers of people would obey the Gospel. G.C. Brewer tells of the first time he ever saw and heard Larimore. Brewer was ten years old and living at that time in Florence, Alabama. He and his brother had walked four miles from their home to Mars Hill. He describes the occasion:

We walked around the sacred spot; drank from the clear, cold bubbling spring; waded in the limpid brook and lounged under the spreading trees while we waited for the great preacher to come out where we could see him. When he finally came, we stood awed and at attention till he passed into the house (the old foundry). We then went in and got seats near a window and waited. After a little while a young man about twenty-six years old, with red hair and a red mustache—who, as I later learned, was Leon K. Harding—announced a song in the "Christian Hymns." It was "Drifting Down the Stream of Time." Such a wonderful singer I had never before heard. Then one or two other songs were sung and brother Larimore preached. His text was Ephesians 2:9-10. "By Grace Are Ye Saved" was the theme. I was lifted out of myself and transported to the glory world. The sad, serene, sweet face of the speaker seemed aglow with earnestness and love for the people. The full, resonant, well-modulated voice filled the old building and vibrated with pathos as the most chaste and beautiful syllables popped and scintillated and the sentences flowed out in rhythmical regularity and almost musical cadences. As I sat by the window and could look out into the bright summer sunlight and up to a beautiful turquoise sky above, with here and there a fleecy cloud floating in a sea of blue, I thought the world more beautiful than ever before. I felt that in some way God was smiling down upon me and saying: "Yes, I love you. I want you to be happy. Do you hear my servant speaking? He is telling you about my grace and mercy; that prayer in Gethsemane, that death on the cross. O, that moves you to tears, but tears of gratitude and joy. I know you love me and want to serve me, and I am going to help you. You will one day preach my gospel as this my servant is now preaching it."[24]

## Chapter V

# A Man of Peace and Purity

It might accurately be said that "preach the word" was T.B. Larimore's motto, so often did he use the expression. He said:

My position is: preach the word wheresoever and whensoever Providence directs or duty demands. Always hew to the line, but never hack toes or chop fingers intentionally.[1]

No man was more gentle and non-combative in his preaching than T. B. Larimore. S. P. Pittman tells the following story:

In Hickman County, Tennessee, he was preaching once, I suspect in a protracted meeting, and a preacher of the denominations disagreed with brother Larimore on some point or points. Before closing the service, brother Larimore asked whether anyone had something to say. This preacher arose and began to argue. He said, "Brother Larimore said so and so, but my Bible says otherwise." For a little while he continued. When there was a lull, brother Larimore said, "Is that all?" "Yes," the man replied. Then Larimore said calmly, "Let us stand and be dismissed." On the surface one might think Larimore acted cowardly and that he had failed to heed Jude's instruction to "contend earnestly for the faith." What a mistake to interpret Jude as advocating a disputatious spirit. In silence and reticence and love and long suffering we may effectually be contending for the faith.[2]

Larimore never wanted to be found guilty of encouraging division or disunity. He felt that it was the plain duty of Christians to abandon and abolish everything but this one body, which is the church, and "keep the unity of the spirit in the bond of peace" in this one body. The formation, operation, and propagation of ecclesiastical organizations, denominational institutions, and partisan brotherhoods in religion produce strife, contentions, animosities, alienations, envyings, and rivalries among Christians; these negative elements inevitably lead to open divisions, which engender an ugly partisan spirit in the body of Christ. The logical effect and constant tendency of the truth of God are to disintegrate and dissolve everything but the "one body in Christ," the church, of which every Christian is a member, whether or not he so much as knows of the existence of anything but the one body in the way of religious institutions. The following comment from Larimore offers a case in point:

> They claim and charge that I preach against certain things, but never name them. I simply "preach the word," "unlearned questions avoid," meddle not with other men's matters, and exhort all to "walk in the light," to simply take God at his word—that is, believe what he says, do what he commands, become and be what he requires, live as he directs, and trust him for what he promises. That's all there is in that—absolutely all. My preaching is Bible preaching. I never try to prove any point in preaching save by the Bible. I simply tell what the Bible says, and then tell them that settles that.[3]

"Brother" Larimore, as nearly everybody called him (not in a restricted or denominational sense, but as an expression of broad and universal brotherhood in Christ) was a representative Christian. People differed in opinion regarding his gifts of oratory, profundity of thought, thoroughness of scholarship, breadth of intellect, and orthodoxy of faith; but all who knew him believed implicitly in his depth of piety, honesty of purpose, sincerity of convictions, and godliness of life.

J. T. Spaulding of Nashville, Tennessee, as quoted by F. D. Srygley, says:

> I have known T. B. Larimore several years, and I regard him as one of the greatest men I have ever known. He is a pure, earnest Christian man who loves God and his fellow men....Everybody who comes in contact with him loves him.[4]

Larimore had a tremendous capacity for love. He entertained pure thoughts; consequently, his words and behavior were chaste. His one consuming ambition in life was to live as the Lord wanted him to live and tell "the sweet, sad story of Jesus." His motto of life was to "Follow peace with all men, and holiness without which no man can see the Lord." After he recovered from a serious illness, he wrote F. D. Srygley the following, which reflects the goodness of his heart:

My faith has never been stronger; my hope has never been brighter; my head has never been clearer; my heart has never been calmer; my life has never been purer. I love all; I hate none. My love for some lifts my soul into the realm of the sublime. I am willing to die today; I am willing to live a thousand years, to tell the old, old story of Jesus and his love. My friends are dearer to me; associations with them sweeter to me; my sympathy for suffering souls is stronger; my love for all the pure, the true, the beautiful, the good, and the sublime—from the bud, the blossom, the babe, up to Him from whom all blessings flow—is truer, tenderer, sweeter, than ever before...Truly I am debtor to all. I sleep soundly, dream sweetly, and "rejoice evermore."[5]

On another occasion Larimore said:

I believe I tell "the truth, the whole truth, and nothing but the truth," when I say I have never done what I believed to be wrong, never refused to do what I believed my duty demanded. My conscience is as clear tonight as when I slept in my mother's arms. I am sure that is true. Without a clear conscience, I could not endure to live, I could not dare to die. Every day of my life is a day of solemn endeavor with me to keep my heart pure and my conscience clear, to be and to do good.[6]

On December 31, 1895, Larimore wrote F. D. Srygley a letter in which he stated he was listing "a few of my life rules...which I hope to strictly observe" in the years to come. These rules, which indicate his great desire to be good and pure, follow:

(1) Be kind; (2) be meek; (3) be true; (4) be humble; (5) be gentle; (6) be polite; (7) be patient; (8) be earnest; (9) be hopeful; (10) be careful; (11) be faithful; (12) be cheerful; (13) be grateful; (14) be generous; (15) be prayerful; (16) be courteous; (17) be unselfish; (18) be thoughtful; (19) be industrious; (20) be consecrated; (21) be conscientious; (22) always do right; (23) do as much good as possible; (24) do as little evil as possible; (25) eat to live, not live to eat; (26) if possible, be perfectly pure; (27) if not, be as pure as possible; (28) always make the best of the situation; (29) be clean body, soul, and spirit—clean in thought, in word, in deed—always clean; (30) conscientiously consecrate all to Christ—head, hand, heart, body, soul, spirit—time, tongue, talent—mind, muscle, money—consecrate all to

Him who gave his very life to ransom a recreant, lost, and ruined race.[7]

In another letter he wrote the following words—words which few men would dare to write:

> Many have been my mistakes, and to me, some of them marvelous; but I am not conscious of having ever done anything that I believed to be wrong. To this, there is no exception. As I approach the tomb, I fear no danger, I dread no death. Not death, but dying; not the judgment, but the grave—the lonely, gloomy grave—do I dread. I fear not the eternal future. Which should I fear? "The Lord is my shepherd." The Lord is my shield. The Lord is my strength and my Savior. My title is perfectly clear.[8]

In 1890, Larimore made a visit to the old Franklin College, from which he had graduated many years before under the tutelage of Tolbert Fanning. A few days later he wrote in a letter about that visit and the sadness which it brought to his heart. Among other things he said:

> I hate no one. I am sure I love all in the sense in which the Lord demands that I love all. Nor man, nor beast, nor bird would I

harm. I sincerely sympathize with the whole
human race, with all things that can suffer or
be sad. I would draw no invidious compar-
isons; I would speak disparagingly or disre-
spectfully of none. I cherish no unkind feeling
toward any person, place, or thing. I know no
preacher who cannot be helpful to me, if I will
listen diligently to what he may say.[9]

T. B. Larimore sought to teach purity, not
only by precept but also by example. "Keep thyself
pure" is an admonition given by Paul to the
beloved young preacher, Timothy. It was a deep
conviction with Larimore that this admonition
must be heeded by all who preach the gospel. In
this connection he wrote:

I have no right, nor has any other mortal who stands as a dying man in the presence
of dying men, women and children, preaching
godliness in the name of the Lord Jesus Christ,
to have any habit that the purest, sweetest,
cleanest Christian mother in all the earth cannot consistently and conscientiously com-
mend to her children. There is no exception to
this—none. A preacher is not necessarily better than any other member of the body of
Christ. If he imagines himself to be better than
his brethren, because of the position he occupies—imagines he is a kind of "reverend,"

"divine," or semi-"divine," connecting link between ordinary Christians and divinity indeed—that is proof positive that he is not as good as humble Christians whom he regards as his inferiors. All of us whether in the pulpit or out of it, should seriously consider the question of duty and destiny, of influence and responsibility; and never forget that we have solemnly agreed to try to be better, purer, cleaner, more like Jesus, than we are.[10]

On one occasion Larimore wrote: "If the church would purify itself, beginning with the pulpit—repent, reform, and be clean—the pulpit would be a power irresistible: the church, an army invincible."

It was the custom of Larimore to preach a series of sermons in which he stressed, with special emphasis and force, the necessity of Christians being pure and chaste and clean—free from all bad habits. He used as his text Romans 12:1, "I beseech you therefore, brethren, by the mercies of God, that ye present your bodies in a living sacrifice, holy, acceptable unto God, which is your reasonable service." He was never known to have delivered this particular series of sermons without many of the hearers resolving to give up some bad habit or habits. At one of his meetings in Texas, a member of the church said, "I believe brother Larimore will preach on Romans 12 throughout his series of meetings, unless I give up the use of tobacco." So he vowed to give it up.[11]

In a letter to a friend Larimore wrote:

> I really do not know which I consider the greater curse, grog or tobacco. When I see a man who has a wife who ought to have a husband, and children who ought to have a father, drinking himself to death, I think grog is the curse of curses. When I see young men and little boys, in broad daylight, puffing poisonous smoke into the faces of decent men and women and innocent little children, and remember this very habit begets a thirst for the fiery waters of death and destruction, I think tobacco is the curse of curses. When I see both, I think they are twin curses. My candid conviction is—if there is any distinct difference—tobacco is a greater curse than grog; as it sometimes "dips" and "brushes" the mother, and "smokes" the little ones, who have inherited the vitiated tastes of their parents, while yet they nestle in, or stand on the edge of the home nest, too young to venture into the deadly darkness of a grogshop.[12]

In the September 26, 1907 issue of the *Gospel Advocate*, there appeared a question directed to David Lipscomb regarding whether a Christian can chew or smoke tobacco "inside the limits of the revealed will of God." Lipscomb responded by saying, "A Christian ought not to spend time or money on that which is filthy or injurious, as these practices are." In a lengthy article in the same issue of the *Advocate*, Lipscomb boldly condemned the use of tobacco along with whiskey.[13] After reading this article, Larimore wrote a letter of commendation to Lipscomb, mailing it from Toronto, Canada. He said in part:

> I have been reading your writings for forty years, and I believe I have never read a better article from your pen than the one in the Gospel Advocate of September 26, on tobacco and other abominations. That the use of tobacco is an abominable abomination need not be said—it says itself.[14]

Larimore lived in such an atmosphere of purity and goodness that he had no fear whatsoever of death. From a western city in the midst of a revival, with the burden of labor and cares heavy on his heart, he wrote to F. D. Srygley:

> "Some sweet day" I'll breathe my last. When you tell the world I am gone, please tell them I was ready, willing and anxious to go; that I dreaded not death; that I fought and fell believing I was on my journey to the

best and brightest place. I never doubt that. I hope it is not egotism, for I feel as little as an atom. I hope it is simply faith sublime, but I no more doubt that I am to be eternally happy as any angel in existence than I doubt the existence of Jehovah himself. That, in my mind, is eternally settled. Conscious of my own littleness, I do my very best, always, everywhere, and under all circumstances, to do all that duty demands—do it with all my might—and do nothing else. So shall it ever be. I want you to know that. My conscience is clear always—never an exception. While I have often come short of duty's demands, and frequently gone beyond the limits of right, I have never done so intentionally.[15]

Larimore not only believed in personal purity and goodness of heart and life, but he also believed and taught that this was the only way for Christians—all Christians—to live. He impressed these things, not only upon the minds of his audiences throughout the land, but also upon members of his own family. The first marriage in his family occurred on December 30, 1897. His gift to the bride, "Dedie," —his oldest daughter—was a Bible he had used in evangelistic meetings. The inscription was as follows:

MARY D. LARIMORE,           MARY L. GEORGE,
December 30, 1897, 2 P.M.     December 30, 1897, 4 P.M.

My daughter: Friends and loved ones excepted, this "blessed Bible," that has been my constant companion so long, is the dearest thing on earth to me, "more precious than gold"; and now I sadly and gladly give it to you, my precious daughter, praying that you may always lovingly "walk in the light" of this precious book—walk in the love light of God's eternal truth—and that the Lord almighty may graciously grant and give up all the desires of your pure heart till, at the peaceful close of a long and useful life, he shall call you home to reign and rejoice in glory with Jesus our Savior forever. Your father, T.B. Larimore [16]

By and by, Larimore was known far and wide for his accomplishments and for his exemplary life. His ability was lauded; his sincerity and purity were accepted without question.

David Lipscomb wrote to a brother who had complained of unjust, unkind treatment from churches and brethren:

You are not alone in having felt the sting of unkindness in churches and brethren. I have felt that sting for myself and others. I

am glad to be able to say I have felt it frequently and as keenly for others as for myself.
I am unselfish in this. The very brethren who
are the most popular feel the sting of unkindness as keenly as others. Brother Larimore, for
instance, has been praised as much as any
one. I sometimes tremble for him, lest the
praises ruin him. But he is of a tender, shrink-
ing temperament, and feels unkindness so
keenly that I feel for him most keenly when
he suffers unkindness. He is called on to suffer frequently....He is so shy of controversy
that sometimes we hardly know where to
place him, but know he will not overstep the
bounds of scriptural authority.[17]

One reader of this comment tried to con-
vince Larimore that Lipscomb had dealt him a
heavy blow. But peace-loving and self-effacing
Larimore was not at all convinced that Lipscomb
intended his observations to be hurtful. "I know,"
Larimore wrote, "whatsoever it might be, it was
done in love, by a true friend, for my good, and that
I should be grateful for it."[18] He refused to consider that there was a "blow" in Lipscomb's statement. It was rather "praise." Larimore related that
Tolbert Fanning had praised him many years
before, when he said: "He will never run off after
anything new. He will never depart from the faith.

He will never disgrace the cause of Christ." Larimore continued by concluding:

> These things are my strongest stay. How can I fall, loved and praised and trusted as I am? What a robber I should be! Tolbert Fanning, David Lipscomb, F. D. Srygley, and thousands of others—friends who "tremble" when they even imagine I'm in danger! It should certainly be practically impossible for me to fall with such a host about me. These things sustain, strengthen, save me. May the Lord love and save my friends.[19]

How did Larimore gain such a strong hold on the hearts of those with whom he lived and labored? One might as well ask, how did John become "the beloved disciple" of the Lord? There were among the twelve, doubtless, other souls as loyal, brave, and true as John; others as well fitted as he to meet the dangers and difficulties that confronted those who followed the Savior, and as ready as he to die in defense of Christ and his cause. He "knew what was in man," understood them all, loved them all, and selected for special work those best suited to that work; but he found in the gentle, affectionate nature of John something that especially appealed to him—something that met and satisfied the longing in his heart for human love and sympathy. He appreciated the

strength, boldness, and fidelity of Peter and committed to him the "keys of the kingdom," thus
making him a leader among the brethren. But as he
hung agonizing on the cross, it was to John's care
that he commended his heartbroken mother,
knowing the depths of the devotion and the tenderness and the sympathy of that beloved disciple's heart.

Human hearts naturally and readily respond
to love, sympathy, and gentleness. Love, "the greatest thing in the world," is the power that must save
the world; sympathy, to be a perfect plant, must be
deeply rooted in the soil of love; and tenderness is
the perfect flower of that perfect plant. There are
many men whom we love for their work's sake and
honor for their devotion to the truth; and yet we
would never turn to them in any hour of sorrow
because their love for humanity, deep and true
though it may be, has never developed the perfect
plant and flower of sympathy and tenderness.
Having suffered long and suffered much, Larimore
knew how to sympathize with the suffering and
the sorrowing—with the light-hearted and happy,
too; and in every great event of love, those who
knew him turned to him confidently, sure of find-
ing the solace and the sympathy they sought.

Larimore received hundreds of letters which
breathed the spirit of love and tenderness; no wonder, for he himself wrote hundreds of such letters.
On a birthday occasion he wrote:

Nearly everybody has always been good to me. I think I could count the exceptions I remember on the fingers of one hand and have some fingers left. If I have treated anybody badly I herein and hereby make all amends I can. I know I have no grudge against anybody, and I'm glad of that. Long ago I was in dreamland with my boyhood friend, Dan Deakins. He was troubled because he thought I had ceased to love him and was no longer his friend. Embracing him as tenderly as I could, I said: "No mortal shall lose an enemy when I die." That seemed to soothe and satisfy him—and it waked me. But, sleeping or waking, that is the sincere sentiment of my heart.[20]

CHAPTER VI

# HIS LATER YEARS

Led by Providence and lured by voices of need to far corners of this nation, T. B. Larimore spent nearly all of his time in evangelistic work. Only in his last years did he accept offers for prolonged arrangements to serve congregations. Before that final phase of his eminent life, the only exception to his exclusive devotion to evangelism was a period of two years, 1889 and 1890, which he spent with the Floyd and Chestnut Street church in Louisville, Kentucky. His letter to the Floyd and Chestnut church in acceptance of their invitation is so revealing and so entirely characteristic of the man that it is herewith quoted in full:

Mars' Hill, Near Florence, Ala.

Aug. 20, 1888.

My Dear Brethren, Sisters—Friends: Many thanks for your patient waiting and watching and persistent pleading. May the Lord abundantly bless you all.

Duty demands of me a definite answer to your earnest call and many blessed letters assuring me of your love, confidence, and esteem, as well as your unanimous and most earnest desire for me to live, love, and labor with you the remnant of my days; and, also, your perfect willingness and enthusiastic anxiety to do any thing and every thing reasonable and right that may be suggested by me, provided only that I will consent to come to Louisville to try to lead you on to victory in the service of the Lord. "The Lord willing," I will try, if I can. By showers of letters and storms of enthusiastic—not to say extravagant—assurances received from many members of your tried, trusty, and true army (body, congregation), I am practically endowed with almost absolute power to dictate terms, specify and fix amount of salary, select a home, etc., etc., with many positive assurances that my will shall ever be your pleasure. Many, many thanks.

This and similar cases, constituting almost a continuous and sometimes resistless stream for yours have long puzzled me. At home and abroad the pressure has been bewildering. I just simply cannot under-stand these things—these mysterious things. They must be solved for me, if ever, beyond the deep, dark, dreaded river. For many years, considering the brevity of the time of my sojourn on the earth, I have been thus importuned, salary suggested being anywhere from—well, I must not give you the figures. They would appear embarrass-ingly boastful, extravagant, and unreason-able. Even now, in answer to a call on my table, I could, with much more ease than I can write this long letter, secure a salary "during life or good behavior," greater than any previously offered me—greater than I am willing to express. And still the calls continue to come; "but none of these things move me, neither count I my life dear unto myself, so that I might finish my course with joy, and the ministry, which I have received of the Lord Jesus, to testify the gospel of the grace of God," where I can do the most good. My financial condition, of which few are informed, is such that, while I do not love money, I need it, and worldly wisdom sug-gests the "the-longest-pole-knocks-the-per-simmon" policy; but I have promised to accept no call in preference to that of

Louisville, and I do not regret it. Of course, the greater the salary, the greater the relief, and, probably, the greater the good I might be able to do; but I am not "up at auction," and shall certainly not take advantage of the suggestion—"State what salary will bring you." As previously intimated, I do not know why my services are in such demand; but honestly believe I am greatly overrated. Many thousands certainly estimate me far, very far above my intrinsic worth and real merit. This may be, in part, because I love, sympathize with, and feel a deep interest in, everybody. This seems to be perfectly natural with me. Indeed, I cannot understand how it can be otherwise with any one. If I know myself, I possess no wondrous ability, either natural or acquired. A certain preacher said when they voted to call me to the congregation to take the charge there, there were but two or three dissenting votes. When they voted to let me leave, there was not one.

Now, suppose I come to Louisville, and after trying me a few weeks or months, you unanimously agree with me—your eyes are being opened by experience—as to my ability. Then what? "What shall the harvest be?" This is a very serious matter with me, and without pride, affectation or selfishness,

I am writing the sincere sentiments of my anxious heart, as they present themselves, as rapidly and accurately as I conveniently can. "The Lord willing," you may expect me—not my family, but me alone—to reach Louisville, ready for work—to "do the work of an evangelist"—not later than January 1, 1889, provided you—all of you—do, and continue to, so desire, and Providence does not appear to point out a different path of duty for me to pursue; but you are perfectly free to make other arrangements with any one—and you will concede the same privilege to me—even to the very day mentioned—January 1, 1889. I expect to come, if at all, without any pledge or promise of salary—to do as I have always done, trust those who trust me. If you can trust me for the preaching, I can certainly trust you for the pay. With the very few exceptions, and these always under the most trying circumstances, in all my work, I have fought for truth and righteousness without money and without price, in the sense of pledge or promise. I have often said nay to a generous proposition to guarantee me a liberal salary, and "so say I now again" to you. Please let it be definitely understood and never forgotten, that either party may, with perfect propriety, at any time, without explanation or previous intimation, sever our relation as evangelist and congregation—thirty days meeting all the demands of our engagement just as completely as thirty years. Let us all remember this. Please prepare me a home—a home. Much, almost all, depends on this. Of course, I should have—must have, to succeed—a comfortable commodious, quiet, well-lighted, well-ventilated room, properly furnished—a preacher's home and study—table, desk, book-case, and other essential helps and conveniences—in a pleasant part of the city. All my surroundings should be such as to make me feel perfectly free and easy—these things are of the greatest importance. It is neither convenient, prudent, nor proper, of course, for me to select my home. That is your province, privilege, and, I am sure, will be your pleasure. There are many among you whom it will afford the greatest pleasure to attend to all these things. I want to do, and you want me to do, my very best. To be unpleasantly situated in any respect, or to lack any thing, would necessarily, inevitably and constantly tend toward universal disappointment. However, this is not my business, but yours, and that assures me that the location, selection, and preparation are absolutely certain to approximate perfection. Well, "what I have written I have written," and I desire all the congregation—every member—to hear it, understand it, and fully comprehend the situation, then, if there be not perfect unanimity in an earnest and enthusiastic anxiety for me to live, love and labor with you—with, for the among you to "do the work of an evangelist"—to "contend earnestly for the faith which was once delivered to the saints"—let that settle the question. I could not consistently consent to either come or stay without believing the earnest, anxious desire of the congregation for me to do so to be unanimous. Have not too high hopes. Be not too sanguine of signal success. "Be not deceived." I may offer you "warmed-over" dishes, dry and dusty; hash made of stale scraps, crumbs and fragments from our former feast, when I tried to spread before you about all I had in store. Bear in mind "blessed are they that expect little, for they shall not be disappointed." It may be possible for me to occupy the happy home your hearts and heads and hands will prepare for me earlier than January 1, 1889; but no such promise is made. Give the place to another at any moment if you wish. I love you and appreciate your enthusiastic call; but have never sought the position you tender me, nor any other. I still seriously doubt my ability to do the work you desire me to do; but, the Lord willing, I will try, and if I fail, the failure will be mine.

Gratefully, affectionately and fraternally,

T.B. Larimore[1]

Serious prayer and thought also led to other changes in the life and direction of T. B. Larimore. On January 1, 1911—"the first day of the week, the first day of the month, the first day of the year, and almost the first hour of the morning—seven o'clock," T. B. Larimore and Miss Emma Page were united in marriage, in Nashville, Tennessee. Their wedding trip took them on an evangelistic tour, "from Maine to Mexico and from Canada to Cuba."

Miss Page was, throughout her life, a highly capable and productive Christian lady in her own right. She had been a stenographer with one of Nashville's leading law firms for a number of years. After the death of F. D. Srygley in 1900, she had taken over the task of editing *Letters and Sermons of T. B. Larimore.* At the same time, and for a number of years, she edited "Children's Corner" in the *Gospel Advocate.* This she continued to do, for some time, after her marriage. In their time together, the Larimores never really established a home of their own. Their home was anywhere and everywhere that Larimore's preaching took them.

Emma Page Larimore shared with her husband involvement in writing for publications. This was an aspect of his service that might be overlooked because of his reputation for great evangelistic preaching. During his sojourn in Washington, D.C., he wrote regularly for the *Gospel Advocate*, under the caption, "Words from Washington." In his articles, he described public buildings and other places of interest in that great city. After moving to California, he continued to write for the *Gospel Advocate*, changing his "Words from Washington" to "Greetings from the Golden Gate." Then, after moving to Southern California, he wrote "Greetings from the Golden West." In addition to writing for the *Gospel Advocate*, he sent frequent contributions to *Firm Foundation* in Austin, Texas, and *Christian Leader* of Cincinnati, Ohio.

Larimore continued to answer calls to evangelistic fields. However, his many-faceted interests and his diverse abilities constantly drew him in the direction of other endeavors. Sometimes the old teaching fever would lay hold on him, and he would plan to establish a school in which young men should be trained to carry on the preaching of the gospel when he and his contemporaries would be forced to give it up; still he was an evangelist, first and foremost. But in 1916, at the insistence of N. B. Hardeman and A. G. Freed, Larimore moved to Henderson, Tennessee and for a time taught young preachers at Freed-Hardeman College. Of that experience N. B. Hardeman wrote:

> I was a member of his class, and no man ever gave better or more practical lessons than he did. I can never forget his expressions and appearance before an audience. His talks at our chapel exercises were among the best he ever delivered.[2]

It was likely that, in campus and classroom situations, many people glimpsed facets of Larimore's nature not generally known. Most often the serious side of the teller of that "sweet, sad story" was seen. Yet it would be a great mistake to conclude, or to leave the impression, that he was always of a totally sober disposition or that he lacked a sense of humor. He actually possessed a keen appreciation for good humor, and he made a jolly companion whenever he thought it prudent to indulge a spirit of social levity.

He told with great relish the story of an old janitor in a city church who said: "I have heard every sermon that has been preached in this church for the past forty years, and thank God I am a Christian still."

He also enjoyed the story about a preacher who wrote a prayer and read it on the special occasion of a railroad meeting. An old Negro man was heard to observe after that opening prayer, "Well, I lay dat's de firs' time de Lawd bin writ' to 'bout de railroad!"[3]

His old teacher, Tolbert Fanning, shared a story that Larimore especially enjoyed. It concerned an old servant of General Andrew Jackson. Fanning, after listening to the old black man tell the many wonderful things "Old Mas' Jackson did when he fit the Britishers at New'rleans," gravely asked: "Do you think your old Master Jackson will go to heaven, uncle?" The old man aptly expressed his faith in General Jackson's strongest point when he quickly answered, "I doan know sah! But if he set 'is head to go, I guess he be mighty apt to git dah."[4] Larimore liked to cite bits of applicable humor. In giving some suggestions to a friend in poor health, he closed his letter by saying: "Josh Billings said the Scripture which says, 'It is more blessed to give than receive' has reference to advice on medicine. I propose to give you both; take or not just as you please."[5]

People who knew Larimore best testify to his enjoyment of good, clean, wholesome fun. Mr. and Mrs. Barnes, members of the church in Washington when brother Larimore was there, recalled how much he enjoyed telling humorous anecdotes.[6]

After his brief tenure in the classroom at Freed-Hardeman, Larimore once more set forth on the evangelistic trail, accompanied by his wife. Indeed, the two of them "went everywhere, preaching the word." His evangelistic work took them into nearly all the Southern states, to Canada, to Detroit, to Washington, D.C. They spent several winters in Florida—in Gainesville, Dade City, and Avon Park; and they labored for several winters in San Antonio and Uvalde, Texas. After visiting California in 1911, they did not return to that state until 1918. For several years thereafter they crossed the continent twice a year, spending the winters and springs in California, the summers and autumns in the East. In California, Larimore preached in various places, and in 1920, the Larimores went to Berkley to live.

He preached in San Francisco for a congregation made up of residents of that city's east side of the Big Bay; also, for the cities of Berkley, Oakland, Alameda, and Richmond. In 1922, a decision was made to start a congregation in Berkley, where brother Larimore had preached many times in the city hall on Sunday evenings. On April 9, 1922, the Berkley church met for the first time, and, as an encouragement to the new work, the entire congregation of the San Francisco church crossed the bay to attend the services.[7]

In 1922 Larimore was invited to Washington, D.C., to conduct a month's meeting. After the meeting, the members of the church prevailed upon the Larimores to remain in Washington and help advance the cause of Christ in that great city. During his stay of three years, he made many friends, and the fellowship grew day by day. While there he preached in New York, Richmond, Virginia, and points in Pennsylvania. At that time W. S. Long, then living in Washington, wrote the following in the *Gospel Advocate*:

> We were together daily for years, and this association revealed to me his master mind, his noble spirit, his humility, and his courage. He lived daily so close to God and had such strong faith in his word that all who heard him preach were drawn nearer to God and made to tremble at the thought of judgment day. Men in every walk of life were made to tremble and to reverence God when they heard T. B. Larimore preach the Bible as he alone could preach it. One United States Senator said: "I go to hear Mr. Larimore preach because I love his reverence for the Holy Scriptures and the sincerity and power with which he quotes the word of God."[8]

In October, 1925, Larimore resigned his work as minister of the Washington church, and he and Mrs. Larimore returned to California, locating in Berkley. Brother Larimore preached for the church there about two and one-half years, becoming very much interested in helping the congregation to secure a building. His dream was realized when a church home was occupied for the first time on January 1, 1928.[9]

In June of 1928, the Larimores left Berkley for Southern California, locating in Santa Ana. Larimore, however, preached regularly for the church in Fullerton, eleven miles away. In addition to his regular work at Fullerton, he continued to preach for various congregations in Southern California, at their annual all-day meetings, an "institution" peculiar to that section. Each congregation had at least one all-day, dinner-on-the-ground meeting each year, with other congregations within automobile or train reach being invited and expected to attend if at all possible. These meetings promoted harmony and fellowship, good will and cooperation among the churches.

The summer and fall of 1928 was a very busy and happy period for the Larimores. He held three meetings during that time: with the Broadway and Walnut church in Santa Ana, beginning in June; with the church in Fullerton, beginning in July; and in November with the Sichel Street church, Los Angeles, where he had conducted many meetings in the past, and where he always delighted to preach.

Into the midst of that period of gratifying success and personal satisfaction, personal tragedy intruded, as it will, to remind of human frailty and the brevity of life. In October of 1928, his son William Herschell was killed in an automobile accident near Florence, Alabama. When the news of Herschell's untimely death reached Larimore in far-off California, he sent a telegraph to Virgil:

> Terrible telegram received causing grief inexpressible, but we rejoice and are glad he was prepared to go. He was a Christian indeed, in whom there was no guile, almost peerless in stature and strength. He was a soul sincere that feared God and knew no other fear. Affectionately, Your father, T. B. Larimore.[10]

Later, in the *Gospel Advocate*, he made an effort to describe his indescribable feelings:

> Of Herschell, as of Absalom, it may be safely said, "From the sole of his foot to the crown of his head there was no blemish in him." Never till now have I imagined that I felt as David felt when he cried: "O my son Absalom, my son Absalom! would God I had died for thee, O Absalom, my son, my son!"[11]

Though the brevity of life was always within the scope of his awareness, Larimore must surely not have foreseen that occasion when he stood to present his final sermon. He had concluded a meeting with the Sichel Street church on Sunday, November 25. Though his intention was to leave Los Angeles immediately, he was detained for the next week. So on Sunday, December 2, he and Mrs. Larimore went to Sichel Street, expecting to hear E. C. Fuqua preach. However, the strong urging of Fuqua and others resulted in Larimore's preaching at both morning and evening services. In the morning he took one of his favorite texts—Jude 3—as the basis for his sermon. That evening he preached again— "one of the most touching, pathetic sermons I ever heard him deliver"—on Matthew 27:23: "Why, What evil hath he done?" It was the last sermon he was ever to preach.[12] So far as his voicing before others "that sweet, sad story," "the rest was silence."

From Los Angeles, the Larimores returned on December 8 to their home in Santa Ana, both sorely afflicted with influenza. By Monday morning, December 17, Larimore was able to be up. About eleven that morning, he walked outside to the garage; but weakness overtook him, and he fell on a concrete slab, breaking his right hip. He was taken immediately to the Santa Ana Valley Hospital where he remained for seven weeks, with his leg and hip encased in a wire frame designed to hold the broken bone in place. When the frame was removed at the end of six weeks, an X-ray examination revealed that the broken bone had knit and there was a strong probability that he would walk again.

While in the hospital, he received calls, telegrams, cards, flowers, letters, and money from

friends throughout the nation. The hospital atten-
dants all fell in love with the preacher of "patience,
fortitude, and sweetness."

On February 3 he returned to his home.
After he was settled in his cheery room, though
unable to sit up, "he had a quiet, peaceful and
almost happy six weeks." It was believed by every
one that he would be able to walk by July 10, 1929,
his eighty-sixth birthday. Dr. Huffman had ceased
to visit him professionally, though he dropped in
occasionally to see that everything was going well.
Dr. Littell, the osteopathic physician, had cut
down his visit to twice a week—Mondays and
Thursdays.

Sunday, March 17, he seemed somewhat
depressed, which was unusual, for he always
rejoiced when Sunday came. However, on that day,
he enjoyed the private worship of reading, prayer,
and communion. Only Mrs. Larimore was present
for that period of worship.

Monday morning, March 18, he seemed to
feel better than at any time since his injury. While
eating breakfast he reminded Mrs. Larimore of
something she had promised to read to him. He
seemed glad when Dr. Littell showed up about
8:45. When the doctor walked around to shake
hands with him, he exclaimed, "How well you
look!" Larimore replied just as cheerily, "I feel
well." Presently he asked the doctor if he should
move to the other side of the bed to make exami-

nation and treatment easier. He said, "I can move myself." He moved over, with a little help from Mrs. Larimore, and settled himself for the treatment, which he always enjoyed. In a few minutes he said to the doctor, "Wait a little while," and glancing at him, Dr. Littell saw that something was wrong. He called to Mrs. Larimore, "Brother Larimore has fainted," and he began trying to restore him. But the end had come, for the saintly T.B. Larimore was now "asleep in Jesus."

He had fought a long, brave fight, thirteen weeks, almost to the hour; but he had heavy odds against him—the sudden tragic death of his son, Herschell, the past October; a severe attack of influenza, followed quickly by the fall in which his hip was broken; and then the long weeks of lying in bed in the same position, unable to move. It was too great a strain on the heart that had served him faithfully and well for more than eighty-five years.

## CHAPTER VII

# CONTEMPORARY APPRAISALS OF T.B. LARIMORE

When a great man, a good man, dies, those in whose lives he made a difference try to pinpoint the marks of his positive impact and the shapes of his influence. T.B. Larimore was a man of unusual stature and personal force; from an obscure beginning he came to a position of fame and respect from Washington, D.C. to California. His death left mourners throughout the United States. Even more significant a phenomenon is the continuation of praise even into the twenty-first century— praise for a man who selflessly gave his life to education and evangelism. Tributes from people of all walks of life poured in, extolling the virtues of the noted and beloved preacher.

The tributes to Larimore indicate, in large measure, the marked influence of the gospel preaching of the man. One is led to believe, from the weight of proof, that he had a greater influence on the lives of those who knew him and listened to his preaching than any other gospel preacher of modern times.

F.C. Sowell of Columbia, Tennessee, wrote:

I am happy to say I belonged to the group of "Larimore and His Boys" for three years while he taught at Mars Hill College. He was so gentle, kind, and good that one would feel that if everybody in the world were just like him, it would give one a fore-taste of what heaven would be.[1]

C. L. Wilkinson, himself a noted evangelist and a former student of Larimore at Freed-Hardeman College, wrote:

Of all the men with whom I have ever associated, I think of brother Larimore as possessing the greatest faith. I am made bet-ter by his influence. The good he did can never be estimated here.[2]

Ernest Beam, a California preacher who was frequently associated with Larimore in evangelistic work, had the following to say:

> I shall ever cherish a simple commendation of a series of sermons delivered at Berkley, California, brother and sister Larimore attending each service without an exception. I remarked to him that I presumed every man was most effective in his own style, but that I was personally pleased that his style was free from levity. He answered: "I have never used it to win souls, Brother Beam, and I see no reason to change my style now."[3]

E.C. Fuqua, who knew Larimore for many years, wrote:

> T.B. Larimore was great. Christ made him great. He threw himself entirely into the plastic hands of the Savior, and greatness is the inevitable reward for this. He was great in humility, in gentility, in faith, in love. I believe these were absolutely perfect in T.B. Larimore, and to admit this is to acknowledge perfection in the earlier or foundation attainments in the same inspired catalogue. In him I learned that man can be "perfect" if they want to....No spasmodic emotions or

"capers" of the Holy Spirit were ever displayed by T.B. Larimore....His hand of blessing was rich in resources and application. "Silver and gold" had he none, being always a poor man, but "such as he had" he freely administered; and God, who was able, did "make grace abound," so that he "had all sufficiency" with which to do vast good in the world, whose every denizen he loved. He was the personification of love; and can love ever die, when that love is the direct fruit of the Spirit in the human heart?[4]

E.N. Glen, who was baptized by Larimore at the age of twenty-one at the Russell Street church in Nashville, wrote of the purity and goodness of the great preacher's life:

His peerless example of patience and deep humility of spirit, coupled with unsurpassed "godliness and brotherly love," led him far into the path of the "highest heights of holiness," which few men of any age have reached.[5]

F.W. Smith, who preached for the Franklin (Tennessee) church for more than thirty years and who died about a year after Larimore did, wrote in the *Gospel Advocate* a lengthy editorial on the passing of a friend and role model. He said, in part:

To me, he was the most eloquent speaker to whom I ever listened, and I have heard many of the greatest orators of modern time. His voice was deep and smooth and his manner of natural gracefulness. As to command of language, I do not think I ever heard his equal. He could bear his audience on wings of the most eloquent flights far away from earth and earthly things, and then let him down with such ease and grace as not to jar the most sensitive...He knew the Bible, and his sermons, always clothed in beautiful and soul-inspiring eloquence, were replete with Scripture quotations.[6]

A.G. Freed, the well-known and greatly-beloved educator and gospel preacher, wrote:

His faith in God's word was sublime. He believed with all his heart that God would "withhold no good thing from them that walk uprightly." To him, faith in divine providence was as dear as life itself. "He staggered not at the promise of God through unbelief." We still hear his ringing words at the close of a wonderful lesson: "Believe all that God says, do what he commands, be what he requires, and trust him for the promises."[7]

Concerning the educational qualities possessed by Larimore, M.C. Kurfees, who preached for the Haldeman Avenue church in Louisville for more than forty-five years, said:

> Brother Larimore was far from attempting to make any display of superior learning, but he was a well-educated man....He was a very studious man with a manifest and strong desire for the acquisition of knowledge in general, but being one of the best-educated men of his day in the English language, and I am free to say was one of the most polished and accurate in the use of it whom is was ever my privilege and pleasure to hear.[8]

F.L. Rowe, editor of the *Christian Leader*, wrote a tribute to Larimore which was later republished in the *Gospel Advocate*. It said in part:

> In my varied experiences of the Leader I have many times had vexatious questions to thrash out singlehanded. Frequently when I have debated what to do, I have asked myself the question, "What would brother Larimore do?" In truth, I regard him the nearest approach to the Savior of any one I know in life. Nothing ruffled him, and he seemed to be fully persuad-

ed just what he should do and nothing would change his program. I recall one little circumstance that reveals his beautiful and Christlike nature. A certain sister had criticized him for something he had said or done, and brother Larimore listened patiently and without interrupting. When she had finished he said to her: "And is that all, sister?" She replied rather shortly, "Yes." Brother Larimore answerd, "I thank you," and went right on with his work as though nothing had happened.[9]

Wayne W. Burton, a newspaper man, wrote in the Nashville *Tennessean*—later copied in the *Gospel Advocate*—on the occasion of Larimore's death, the following words:

As an evangelist, Elder Larimore was free from all sensational methods, slang, and catch phrases. He was absolutely non-combative and never aroused a warlike feeling or resorted to clerical claptrap or verbal gymnastics for temporary effects. He was devotional by nature and had confidence in the gospel and in men to accept it when presented.[10]

In the Nashville *Banner* appeared these words, which were later published in a memorial issue of the *Gospel Advocate*:

That he was personally known to more people than any other man in the brotherhood from this long period of service and that he had preached more sermons than any other man living was the claim frequently made by religious authors, some of whom advanced the claim that he had probably baptized more people than any minister in the church of Christ for nearly one hundred years. Editors and authors in the religious field had challenged the records of William Hayden, Walter Scott, and Benjamin Franklin, of the period of the Campbells, as well as that of the evangelists, John Allen Gano and John T. Johnson, of the early Restoration movement in the blue-grass region of Kentucky. Gano had immersed nine thousand and eight hundred with his own hands, and Franklin more than ten thousand.[11]

It was not only Larimore's brothers in Christ who saw that which should be held up to praise. Representing admirers/critics from outside the brotherhood is a Baptist preacher, a contemporary of Larimore. He made these interesting observations:

T.B. Larimore, who is one of the most scholarly Campbellite preachers in the South, is closing today a month's meeting in Sherman, Texas. He clings so closely to the exact wording of the Scriptures, and makes such a profound impression against party-ism, that many may be led by him. Here is a sample:

"The Bible says baptism is for the remission of sins; it nowhere says it is for any-thing else." This is the only statement, in four long sermons, I heard him make that I could not accept as true, both as to purpose and meaning. The statement is difficult to prove false; but evidently it teaches baptismal regeneration. Without showing the danger-ous tendency of this statement, I introduce it here, to show how hard it would be to reply to him. I am told he never debates. Like Dr. Gambrell, he considers debating beneath his dignity, I presume....Mark my prediction: Sherman, Whitewright, Benham, and every other town to which he had preached a month will have Campbellism spreading like Johnson grass; and, like Johnson grass, it can never be destroyed, except by digging it up and cultivating something else in its place.[12]

Over seventy years have now gone by since the death of Theophilos Brown Larimore, yet he continues to be highly esteemed and gratefully remembered. He no doubt will become a legend among "Christians only" in much the same way that Abraham Lincoln has become a legend to the

American people and to the world. His name and his memory are bright at his beloved Mars Hill. His almost magical way with words and his inspiring faith and knowledge stir those who know him from his sermons and letters and from shared anecdotes of those who knew him best. Within the story of his life of struggles, of accomplishment, there lies lessons for all who believe the "sweet, sad story" which was his theme and who aspire to go at last to that glorious home that was more real to him than anything in this world.

The following appraisal of T. B. Larimore by S. P. Pittman seems an appropriate way to bid him farewell:

In Washington, D.C. once I passed a man on the sidewalk whose figure and features and face impelled me to turn and look at him again. It was none other than the then famous and fascinating T. DeWitt Talmadge, whose syndicated sermons were read avidly by the American people many years ago.

T.B. Larimore was just such a personality. It was fortunate for the cause of Christ in the post-Civil War period that the subject of this sketch was a happy combination of excellencies. Physique, intellectuality and spirituality were wrapped up in the person of the late T.B. Larimore. We cannot attribute his popularity and success to nature's generosity alone. Like all other human beings he began with zero and with effort ascended by degrees the personal human thermometer.

Some preachers may be called negative characters and some may be called mediocre; but not T.B. Larimore. He was stately, but not proud; dignified, but not stiff; deferential, but not obsequious; an orator, but not a haranguer; scholarly, but not pedantic. Let us mention some of his salient characteristics:

"Hiding behind the cross" is, with us, a trite expression, yet quite appropriate. If ever a great preacher of the Gospel succeeded in doing that very thing, it was the apostle Paul. And yet, in the introduction to the Book of Romans it is impossible to keep him from "peeping" from behind the cross and thus he exhibits his own attitudes and emotions, as it were, inadvertently. The same could be said of T.B. Larimore. With no attempt to advertise his own ability or superiority or godliness, his poise and presence and voice expose these characteristics. Few, since the days of Alexander Campbell, could hold the crowds that Larimore held, or the attention of an audience as he could. His long meeting in Sherman, Texas is an adequate proof. He must have been an ardent thinker and student, both in and out of the schoolroom. His auditors got the thrill of the finished product, his sermon, without realizing the indefatigable labor he must have expended in preparing for the delivery.

No doubt early in life he learned to be methodical. Could we see behind the curtain, we would be impressed with his methodical ways of doing chores, laboring in the field and studying, which carried over in the preparation, composition and delivery of his sermons. In his living, eating, sleeping, working, he was well-acquainted with regimen.

He was inclined to uniqueness. For example, in his rhetorical expression (for he was a rhetorician as well as an orator) he had his own way of handling the English language that we might term "Larimorean." It is said that his dentist lived in one city, his physican in another (probably some distance away), his watchmaker in still another. The announcement of his marriage the second time is another proof. He was temperate in all things. He was not a heavy eater—no doubt eliminated from the menu things he considered detrimental. In his protracted meetings he did not turn them into feasts. Shortly after the Sunday dinner, he would return to his stopping place for rest, meditation and study, presumably. Sometimes during his second marriage he would be furnished with a room or apartment where his wife could continue to look after his best interests.

He looked after his physical needs sedulously. He probably bordered at times on spending freely. As an example, contrasting him with James A. Harding, who was frugal and self-sacrificing, and would travel by day coach on the train, Larimore would take the sleeper. It might be fair to state here that brother Larimore was usually paid handsomely (for that time) for his services as preacher; and that enabled him to live comfortably. Doubtless reports of his living in luxury were more exaggerated.

As is well known the three most popular kinds of sermons are: (1) Topical, such as on "Faith." (2) Textual, such as John 3:16. (3) Expository, such as reading and explaining a portion or all of Romans 12. No doubt brother Larimore employed all three of these types. We can imagine him as feeling at home in the pulpit in any method. Probably his most potent efforts combined the three in one. You can know that he didn't get far afield in text or topic. He stuck closely to what he proposed to elucidate. He was thoroughly conversant with the word of God, both Testaments. He was a great believer in sticking to the very words of the text. He used illustrations, Biblical and otherwise, but it would have been out of his line to go out of his way so as to get to tell a tale. He was no sensationalist.

In speaking of his combining two or more methods, an example of his practice is in order. When he arose to begin his sermon he prefaced his discourse with the reading (by heart) of Matthew 16:13-20. Using this Scripture as a source or basis he probably got over the first verse of the paragraph. The next night he would rise in his calm dignity and begin again "Now when Jesus came into the parts of Caesarea Philippi" and on and on. Then an exposition of the second verse. Probably a whole week on that rich paragraph.

He was no hobby-rider. None of us can claim total escape from hobbyism, but T.B. Larimore seemed to be about as far from that "disease" as any one in the brotherhood. He probably had decided convictions on many disputed questions, but he was not insistent on his opinions. I remember only one question that he had a decided opinion upon and that he preached from the pulpit. That is, he believed that Jesus was crucified on Thursday, while the usually accepted idea was that it was on Friday.

T.B. Larimore must have known where decisions—in belief and practice— were made, i.e., in the heart, in the inward man. He must have known that love was the determining factor. He seemed to love everybody and in return, everybody loved him—saint and sinner. Perhaps we are too ignorant of the "inner light." He was inclined to mysticism. He never told all he knew. He kept much in reserve while dispensing truth. On more than one occasion he seemed to be a telepathist on the subject of telepathy. When in California, he wrote to an intimate acquaintance living in Denver, Colorado that he expected to come East in two or three weeks, and expected to come by and see his friend, brother King, a tubercular living in Denver. Larimore changed his plan and came a week or so earlier than he anticipated. Coming by Colorado Springs he went up on Pike's peak—73 miles away on an airline. In his invalid's chair King was rolled out upon the porch and looked toward the famous peak and said: "I see brother Larimore on Pike's peak." He was rolled back into the house. Soon a telegram was handed him signed T.B. Larimore, Pike's Peak, Colorado, saying he would see him soon. The time synchronized. Was he miraculous? Perhaps not—just weird. A bosom friend of brother Larimore's died about the first of the present century. Larimore wrote that his friend, F. D. Srygley, had died of a broken heart. Whether any one ever knew what was meant I do not know. Probably brother Larimore himself was the only one who knew the real meaning of his statement.

I have a right to be interested in this great person. He ran Mars Hill College near Florence, Alabama, in which young preachers were educated and trained. When I was born in West Tennessee, my parents had heard brother Larimore preach and admired him. When they picked me out as the preacher (to be) of the family, my people planned to send me to Mars Hill. The school was discontinued. The Nashville Bible School was opened up in 1891. So there is where I went. It is a bit of sentiment on my part when I say that in the fall of 1892, I began to preach in the very house where T.B. Larimore held his first meeting, Burnett's Chapel. It is a pleasant memory to me, that when Larimore was preaching at Fourteenth Street church in Washington, D.C., I made a visit to that city and, on Lord's Day brother Larimore being unwell, I had the privilege of relieving him that day, by preaching for him.

I am reminded of another incident that took place earlier than the one just mentioned. The Lawrenceburg, Tennessee church, strong now, was in its incipiency. They were moving out of the courthouse into their new brick building. Larimore was to hold the first meeting in the new building. It fell to my lot to take his place in this meeting, as he was sick and unable to go. Brother Leon P. Harding, son of James A. Harding, led the singing for the meeting. He was a most excellent song leader. That reminds me to say that the three men who have been ideal to me and who have been so influential in my life were David Lipscomb, James A. Harding, and T. B. Larimore.[13]

# CONCLUSION

In this review of the life of T. B. Larimore, the unquestioned conclusion is that he was no ordinary man. He possessed qualities, characteristics, and endowments that few men are privileged to possess. Larimore is dead, but his influence lives on to bless and encourage future generations. In this connection we think of the familiar words in the last book of the New Testament. "And I heard a voice from heaven saying, write, Blessed are the dead who die in the Lord from henceforth: yea, saith the Spirit, that they may rest from their labors; for their works follow with them" (Rev. 14:13).

A number of years ago, I heard the late George W. Truett preach several times in a meeting at the Druid Hills Baptist church in Atlanta, Georgia. In one of his sermons he mentioned that in his estimation, Horace Bushnell's sermon "Every Man's Life a Plan of God" was the greatest sermon in existence, outside the inspired sermons of the Bible. At that time I had never read Bushnell's sermon. It was not long after that that I was browsing in a second-hand bookstore and ran across a book by Bushnell, *Sermons for the New Life.* I was delighted to observe that the first sermon in the book was the one that Dr. Truett had mentioned. I hastily purchased the volume and read with consuming interest the sermon in question. While I may not place the value upon the sermon that Dr. Truett placed upon it, it is nevertheless a sermon with a tremendous idea.

In a lecture preached at Abilene Christian College in 1938, Paul Southern said, "May I suggest that the world is still waiting for the sunrise of real Christian devotion.[1] "May I suggest" that if mortal man ever yielded to God's plan for man, it was T. B. Larimore. When the sun rose on Larimore, it rose on a man who more nearly yielded to the will of God than perhaps any other man of our time. God had a plan for Larimore's life. It is the concensus of all who knew him that Larimore yielded to God's plan; as a result, life has been richer for countless people.

Larimore believed that Providence protects all who "truly trust God, and lovingly obey him," "as surely, certainly and constantly as Jehovah was ever the shield of Abraham, Peter and Paul."[2] He believed wholeheartedly that God would do everything that he promised to do. Probably J.A. Harding and T.B. Larimore were the strongest believers in special providence among all the preachers of their time. These two men were constantly engaged in the Lord's work. No two men spent less time in idleness or recreation than Harding and Larimore. It is said that Spurgeon was a phenomenon of faith in special providence and a prodigy in the abundance of his labors. All believers in special providence, including Larimore, seem to have an idea that they must devote their time closely in God's service to enjoy the promises of his special care and protection. In a letter to a friend Larimore wrote: "You know I am a firm believer in special providence. Rob me of that belief, and of my belief in the efficacy of prayer, and I am an atheist."[3]

As has been indicated elsewhere in this book, Larimore quoted the Great Commission in nearly every sermon he preached. It was his authority for preaching "the word." It set forth the conditions of pardon for the alien sinner, and too, it gave a promise that the Lord would be with all who preach his word, even to the end of the earth. Larimore believed that the Lord meant what he said—that he would do what he promised.

# Sermons of T.B. Larimore

## The Iron, The Silver, And The Golden Rule

JUDGE not, that ye be not judged. For with what judgment ye judge, ye shall be judged: and with what measure ye mete, it shall be measured to you again. (Surely no man can claim or desire more than this—to buy and sell by the same yardstick.) And why beholdest thou the mote that is in thy brother's eye (little blemishes in your brother's conduct or life), but considered not the beam that is in thine own eye (the greater sin of which you are guilty)? Or how wilt thou say to thy brother, Let me pull out the mote out of thine eye; and, behold, a beam is in thine own eye? Thou hypocrite, first cast out the beam out of thine own eye (get right yourself); and then shalt thou see clearly to cast out the mote out of thy brother's eye (you can consistently criticise him when you get right yourself).

"Give not that which is holy unto the dogs, neither cast ye your pearls before swine, lest they trample them under their feet, and turn again and rend you."

"Ask, and it shall be given you; seek, and ye shall find; knock, and it shall be opened unto you: for every one that asketh receiveth; and he that seeketh findeth; and to him that knocketh it shall be opened. Or what man is there of you, whom if his son ask bread, will he give him a stone? Or if he ask a fish, will he give him a serpent? If ye then, being evil, know how to give good gifts unto your children, how much more shall your Father which is in heaven give good things to them that ask him? Therefore all things whatsoever ye would that men should do to you, do ye even so to them: for this is the law and the prophets." (Matt. 7:1-12) Surrounded by a great throng of people in the plain, and weary of his surroundings for the present, Jesus withdrew from the crowd and ascended to the summit of a little hill nestling with becoming modesty among the mountain of the Land of Promise; and when he had seated himself, his disciples came unto him, and he opened his mouth and taught them the things that constitute the fifth, the sixth, and the seventh chapters of

Matthew—a crown of radiant gems and jewels
rare that have come down through the ages,
sparkling and glittering and flooding the world
with light divine for eighteen hundred years, and
that will continue to brighten our pathway with
wondrous light until we wing our flight among the
stars, provided we become children of the living
God, reduce these principles to practice in our
lives, and prove faithful unto death.

Among these jewels we find the language:
"Therefore all things whatsoever ye would that
men should do to you, do ye even so to them: for
this is the law and the prophets." (Matt. 7:12)

Man is so constituted that rules and regulations, discipline and government, are necessary in
all the relationships of life. Every school must have
its rules, its regulations, its government, its discipline. It is true that there are some arbitrary rules,
as there are some arbitrary teachers; but the existence of arbitrary rules no more argues against the
importance of rules than the existence of arbitrary
teachers argues against the importance of teachers.
Every school must have its rules and regulations,
its discipline and government, and these must be
properly administered and properly respected, in
order that the school may be a blessing to the community and a blessing to mankind.

The church of the living God is a school, all
Christians being pupils, scholars, or disciples in
that school; the sixty-six volumes of the Bible

being the textbooks for these pupils to study, that they may grow in grace and in the knowledge of the truth. Jesus is the great head Teacher—the Teacher of teachers. God is the supreme Head over this divine, spiritual institution, and he has sent the Holy Spirit to his children here to comfort and help them in the study and practice of these wonderful lessons.

But people are never pupils in a school until they have entered the school. There is never a chance for them to be promoted to another grade until they have entered some grade, no chance to enter until they have matriculated, and no chance to have any honor in the school until they have entered it. Just so with this divine institution called "the church." We must, as responsible souls, matriculate in this school, enter it in God's appointed way, and come under the law governing its pupils, in order to be benefited, in order to be entitled to the emoluments and honors connected with this wonderful institution over which God himself presides.

Every army must have its rules, its regulations, its government, its discipline, its tactics, without which a comparatively numberless host may be routed, wrecked, and ruined by a few well-offered, well-equipped, and well-governed soldiers, submissive to the rules, regulations, and tactics of the army, as was demonstrated by the memorable crusades of the tearful, bloody long ago.

The church of God is an army. Jesus is the Leader of that army; God is at the head of the government, directing this army; and every Christian is a soldier of the cross. Hence Paul says: "Fight the good fight of faith, lay hold on eternal life, whereunto thou art also called, and hast professed a good profession before many witnesses." (1 Tim. 6:12) "Thou therefore endure hardness, as a good soldier of Jesus Christ. No man that warreth entangleth himself with the affairs of this life; that he may please him who hath chose him to be a soldier. And if a man also strive for masteries, yet is he not crowned, except he strive lawfully." (2 Tim. 2:3-5) In Eph. 6 we have the soldier's armor spoken of as applied to Christians: the helmet of salvation, the breastplate of righteousness, the shield of faith, the sword of the Spirit—everything connected with the armor of the ancient soldier mentioned as belonging to the soldier of the cross. In Heb. 2:9, 10, the Savior is spoken of as the Captain of our salvation: "But we see Jesus, who was made a little lower than the angels for the suffering of death, crowned with glory and honor; that he by the grace of God should taste death for every man. For it became him, for whom are all things, and by whom are all things, in bringing many sons unto glory, to make the captain of their salvation perfect through sufferings"—the word "captain" being used in the sense of commander in chief, the leader of the Christian hosts, battling for the salvation of souls.

Every family must have its rules and regulations, its discipline and government, in order to be
a blessing to the world, as God would have all families to be. We speak of a well-regulated family—
that is simply a family submissive to good regulations, to good rules, properly administered,
respected, and obeyed. Families must have rules
and regulations to be governed by.

The church of God is a family—God the
Father, Christ the elder Brother, and all Christians
brothers and sisters. "The Spirit itself beareth witness with our spirit, that we are the children of
God." (Rom. 8:16) The Bible authorizes Christians
to call God their Father. This shows that they are
children of God, with Jesus as their elder Brother;
and as all the Christians on this earth are members
of God's family, that family must have its rules of
government.

Every kingdom must have its government.
The church of Christ is spoken of as a kingdom:
"Giving thanks unto the Father, which hath made
us meet to be partakers of the inheritance of the
saints in light; who hath delivered us from the
power of darkness, and hath translated us into the
kingdom of his dear Son; in whom we have redemp-
tion through his blood, even the forgiveness of
sins." (Col. 1:12-14) This divine government, of
course, must have its laws by which it is governed.

Every natural human body must have rules
and regulations governing it—we call them rules

of health—and to the extent that these rules are observed, men have greater prospect of health, happiness, and longevity than those who do not comply with these laws of the human body. The church of Christ is compared to the human body: "So we, being many, are one body in Christ, and every one members one of another." (Rom. 12:5) The same though appears in 1 Cor. 12.

Now, then, since each of these—since the school, since the army, since the family, since the kingdom or government, since the natural human body—must be governed by rules and regulations, these being properly observed in order that proper results may come; and since the church is like all these, and God himself compares it to all these, the conclusion comes with full force, in the light of these illustrations, that the church must have government, must have discipline, must have rules and regulations, to be observed by its members. The church can no more prosper and be the institution God would have it be, without its rules and regulations of government, than a school, an army, or a kingdom can be prosperous without its rules and regulations, its government and discipline. No church can prosper without government.

We should not wonder, then, that Christ submitted to his disciples a rule of life to govern them in their relationship to each other, to him, and to God. Hence Jesus said to his disciples: "Therefore all things whatsoever ye would that men should do to you, do ye even to them" — the royal rule of righteousness, submitted by the Savior to his disciples, to be observed by them and to be observed by his servants until time's knell shall be sounded and the redeemed shall be gathered home.

There are three rules recognized among men that have received metallic names. The first of these in point of antiquity—and, unfortunately, the first in point of numbers, if we consider the men who have submitted to live in accordance with its requirements—is what is known as the "Iron Rule," otherwise called the "Rule of Cain," because Cain, the firstborn human being on the earth—Adam and Eve were made, Cain was born—was the first to make himself notorious by submitting to its demands. This heartless rule is based upon the Satanic principle that might makes right. All the carnage, cruelty, and crime that have cursed the earth for six thousand years, growing out of a spirit of pride, a spirit of selfishness, of greed for gold—justifying and emphasizing Burns' poetic expression, "Man's inhumanity to man makes countless millions mourn"—may be traced with inerring certainty to the shadow of the Iron Rule, the principle that might makes right. From the time that Cain murdered Abel, his soul full of hatred and envy of his innocent brother, no such set has ever stained the earth with blood that has not been committed in obedience to the demands of the Iron Rule. In all the ages there has never been a man, ambitious of conquest, thirsting for personal grandeur and greatness and glory, power and popularity and dominion, who has unsheathed his sword and marched his legions into erstwhile peaceful communities and filled them with the wreck of homes and broken hopes and blighted prospects, that he might add to his own possessions and power and dominion—doing this work for self and prompted to it by sordid, selfish, Satanic motives—who is not worshiping in the shadow of the Iron Rule. It is not necessary for us to single out some characters along that line.

It is not necessary for us to go far back over the hills and plains of the long ago to Alexander, weeping because he could reach no other worlds to bathe them in blood and drench them in tears; to Hannibal, who held Rome under the heel of his tyranny for fourteen years; to Caesar, in his eight years of Gallic wars, laying waste to a once-fair country, slaying or reducing to bondage three millions of her people; to the illustrious Corsican, the adopted son of France, as he crushes kingdoms, overturns thrones, breaks scepters, and plays with crowns as children in the nursery play with toys—it is not necessary to go to these to find worshipers at the shrine of the Iron Rule. In all this favored land we call "our country"—a Christian country—there is not a man called "husband" by a faithful, loving, and dutiful wife, who, forgetful of promises

made in twilight's semisacred hour in the long ago,
or sacred vows made at the hymeneal altar—vows
as sacred and as binding as any oath ever administered beneath the stars—is now a cruel tyrant, to
be feared, instead of the fond, compassionate husband and father, to be revered, who is not as surely a servant of Satan, a worshiper of self at the
shrine of the Iron Rule, as was ever Alexander, or
Hannibal, or Caesar, or Napoleon, or any bloody
tyrant the world has ever seen—a smaller, lesser,
but more contemptible, specimen of the same cruel
class. It does not make any difference what position—ecclesiastical, political, or social—he may
fill; it does not make any difference how phari-
saical he may look, how long he may make his
prayers or his sermons; if that be his character, he
is serving Satan to Satan's perfect satisfaction.
While he may wear the livery of Heaven, he is serving Satan, and not the spotless Lamb of God, who
gave his life to redeem us, who died upon the cross
that we might live. It is not necessary for man to
deceive himself with the idea that he is headed for
heaven because he prays long prayers or preaches
long sermons; for God knoweth the heart, and out
of the heart cometh the issues of life. If the heart is
evil, the life is not pure in the sight of God. But we
can go from the family circle, from the home, shad-
owed by such a cruel tyrant, or from a home that is
blessed by such a husband as that cruel tyrant
should be, to any congregation of Christians, and

in some of these congregations, it may be, we can find specimens of this same class of persons. Whenever we find the "rule-or-ruin," "boss-or-burst," "my-way-or-no-way" man in the church of God, in any congregation of Christians in the service of God, there we find the Iron Rule character, and that man can do more damage to the cause of Christ, occupying a position nominally in the church of Christ, than any seven men of equal power can do, if standing in open opposition to the church of God. Occupying that position gives him a vantage ground that no man without that nominal relationship could ever have. Of course you know, and I know that you know, that I have no reference to the man that stands up, like brave old Elijah of old, for God's right to rule. These two characters—the one who is determined to rule or ruin, boss or burst, have his way or no way, and the man who is ready to do and bear and die for God's right, standing up for his "thus it is written," "thus saith the Lord"—are as far apart as the opposites of limitless space; as far apart as the east is from the west; as far from each other as the deepest, darkest depths of perdition from the highest heights of rapture that canopy the eternal throne of God. The one—the rule-or-ruin man—is a curse to the community in which he lives, so far as his influence is felt; the other, a blessing to all around him, a man that angels admire and that Heaven will receive at last. We may just look around in all the relations of life, and whenever we see a man who, simply because he has the power to do it, lays hold on that which is not his own, who oppresses anybody or robs anybody, then we have an example of those who worship at the shrine of the Iron Rule. If there is a man, be he pope, priest, or preacher, who has taken advantage of some technicality of law or the absence of some important witness whose testimony would have brought truth to light, or the loss of some important paper, to get a decree of court in his favor, and, having got it, has taken property which may be the home and rightful possession of some unfortunate widow and her helpless children, when he knows that according to the eternal principles of everlasting justice he has no right to these things, but holds them simply by the decree of court and under the protection of the strong arm of the law, he is a servant of Satan, worshiping in the shadow of the shrine of the Iron Rule. No decree of court has ever made wrong right. The decree may come from the lowest court in the land, it may be appealed until it reaches the Supreme Court of the United States, and the decision of the lower courts may be upheld to the last; but still, if the first decision is wrong, the last one is wrong, and all the others are wrong. These decisions and decrees cannot make the wrong right. It is presumable, of course, and the general inference is, that the decrees of court are right, or should be, but the decree of court does not make it so; and it is reasonable to believe that there are thousands of people today holding property who know that according to the eternal principles of right and justice the property belongs to others. It matters not what may be their ecclesiastical, financial, political, or social position , they are robbers; trying to get and enjoy the goods of others, they have worse than stolen them; they are Iron Rule people, and there is not grace enough in the bosom of God to save them unless they repent, make restitution, turn to God, and live the Christian life.

I am sure there is no man who would be advertised as an Iron Rule man, and there is no man who will question a single point I have made. You have the right to criticise my logic or my grammar, but I do not believe there is a man here who will criticise the principle I have laid down. There is not a man who would be willing to be advertised as an Iron Rule man. If I should call him out and say, "Here is an example of the Iron Rule man" this audience would consider it a shame, a burning disgrace. It is a strange thing that men of culture and refinement will be for years, willfully, willingly, knowingly, and intentionally, what they would consider it an unpardonable outrage for any man to either publicly or privately accuse them of being, and at the same time and during that time persistently refuse to be what they would like for the whole world to believe they are, when it is a voluntary matter and left for them to say, just as it is left for the sinner to come and be a child of God or not.

The second of these rules in point of antiquity, and one that occupies the halfway point between the deep, dark depths occupied by the Iron Rule and the heights whereon we find the law of Christ, has been called the "Silver Rule"—otherwise, the "Rule of Confucius," because Confucius, a Chinese philosopher, who lived about five hundred years before the birth of the Babe of Bethlehem, embodied this rule in his teachings. The Silver Rule, the Rule of Confucius, is this: "Do nothing to others that you would not have others do to you." All can understand that this is a wonderful improvement on the Iron Rule, a rule of much higher grade than that Satanic and heartless rule; and yet the Silver Rule is very deficient indeed. It is purely negative. It does not actually demand that we do anything. It forbids much, but does not demand anything. It would not allow you to apply a torch to your neighbor's home, but does not require you to stop and spend three minutes in extinguishing the flames, if you should see them doing their dreadful work; it would not require you to stop and save your neighbor's child from the waves, if you saw him drowning, though it would forbid your pushing him into the water. So far as this rule is concerned, a man may step aside and let the suffering suffer, the perishing die, and never violate one single syllable in it. I am sure there is not a man in this audience willing to be classed so low as the worshipers at the shrine of the Silver Rule, living negative lives, living for self, and, while not taking time to injure others, never extending a helping hand to one single son of Adam's race. According to every principle of justice and right, there is no man who has the right to be a Silver Rule man. We are under obligations to help others, to be ready to sympathize with and succor the suffering and needy wherever we go; live to bless ever and curse never, thus obeying the injunction of Him who has said to Christians; "Bear ye one another's burdens, and so fulfill the law of Christ." (Gal. 6:2)

The third, and last, of these rules has been called the "Golden Rule" — otherwise, the "Rule of Christ," because Christ was the author of it. The Iron Rule, the Rule of Cain—"Might makes right"; the Silver Rule, the Rule of Confucius — "Do nothing to others that you would not have others do to you;" the Golden Rule, the Rule of Christ— "Therefore all things whatsoever ye would that men should do to you, do ye even so to them."

We should all rejoice that Jesus, the immaculate Son of God, has given us this absolutely pure rule of life; we should all rejoice that it is our privilege to enter into his service and live according to the demands of this rule; we should rejoice in the thought that to the extent we live the Christian life we are helping the world to live according to this divine principle, this Golden Rule.

I rejoice that I have never come to the conclusion that Golden Rule people are scarce in this
world. I may have too much confidence in my fel-
lowman, and may love my brethren and sisters too
tenderly, constantly, and confidingly; it may be
that I am often deceived by having too much confidence in people wherever I go; but I would rather
be deceived and suffer along this line than to suffer
under the influence of the thought that Golden
Rule people are so scarce in this world that the
safest way is to consider every man a scoundrel
until he proves himself to be a gentleman. All over
this land are Gold Rule men and women, who, to
the extent of their ability, are living up to the rule.
I remember a blessed, good woman who at one
time took a journey to Texas, and on her return
found she had ten dollars more money that she
ought to have. She was worked up about it; she
thought about it, dreamed about it, prayed over it,
and suddenly she thought: "There is just one place
for me to have made this mistake." She remembered that at one place she had to get the ticket
agent to change a bill for her. She quietly wrote the
ticket agent at that place in Texas, "Did your
money balance, or your accounts balance, at the
end of a certain time?" not intimating whether she
had lost fifty dollars or was fifty cents ahead. She
got a polite note from the agent saying that at the
end of that month he was ten dollars short, and
had never been able to make his accounts balance.

She immediately remitted the ten dollars to him in a safe way, received his grateful acknowledgements, and felt easy. Do you say this is not worth relating? It would not be, if all who claim to be Christians were really what Christianity would make them if they would submit to its principles every day. A man with whom I was acquainted amassed a great fortune. Twenty years after his wife died he also died, leaving a son and two daughters. For some reason that has never been satisfactorily explained, he gave his fortune to his son, just leaving enough to his daughters to make the will stand the test. So far as I know, no one knows why he did so. It may be that he wished, like the elder Vanderbilt, to keep his property together; or that he believed his daughters would not know how to manage such fortunes; so he gave it all to the son. The son waited for about forty days after the death of the father, and then came the time for a decision as to what was to be done. We all see that he was confronted by a situation where he had to choose between the three rules. On the Iron Rule principle, he could have told them to get out. You say this would have been Satanic; the Iron Rule is always Satanic. On the Silver Rule principle, he could have said to himself: "These things are mine. If they want to stay here and risk their chances, live of the crumbs that fall from my table, they can stay; but these things are mine." We all know what he would have done if he had decided to go according to the Golden Rule. The forty days having elapsed, he called his sisters into the family room—that room where the hand of the mother had rocked the cradle where each in turn had slept and smiled and dreamed, all unconscious even of the loving mother's heart. He then produced three documents. A lawyer himself, he had called to his aid in preparing these papers all a lawyer's experience along that line.He had made a careful invoice of all the property, and had made three lists of equal value, one-third of the property on each list. He requested the sisters to listen while he read over these lists, and be able to decide what they considered most valuable, the second, and the least valuable. He turned to the older sister, when they had both told him they understood, and demanded that she take first choice. She threw her arms about his neck and begged him not to ask her to do this; but he insisted that she pledge her honor to take the one she really preferred, and she finally did so. The same scene was enacted between him and the other sister, who regretfully and reluctantly took her choice, leaving him one-third. Instead of all the property, he has but one-third; but we can see that in reality he is infinitely richer than if he had all the property and ten times more. He had acted upon the principle of the Golden Rule. I am not sure but there are people who claim to be Christians, who preach longer sermons and offer up longer prayers than patient, polite people ought to have to listen to from such a source, who would not have done as that man did; and yet, sad to say, that man was not a Christian, is not a Christian today, and I think there is little probability that he will ever be a Christian. I am almost sure he was wrecked and ruined along that line long ago by the deception, hypocrisy, sin, and wickedness among those who claim to be children of God. As a lawyer, he had heard false swearing from those claiming to be Christians, and had lost faith in mankind and faith in his Maker, and is destined some day to go into eternity without God and without a hope of the blessings the Father promises to all his faithful children. Such lessons should make us realize the responsibility resting upon us as followers of Christ, and see to it that we never fall short of the requirements of this Golden Rule of life.

I want to touch upon a Bible example. I never like to close without closing on the solid Rock. In Luke 10:25-37, in the story of the good Samaritan, we have a traveler, some robbers, a priest, a Levite, a Samaritan, a lawyer, and the Savior — these seven characters and classes of characters in that beautiful and valuable story— and we have these three rules brought out in it. The robbers were the Iron Rule men. "There are many of us, he is alone; we will rob him, take what he has, and leave him dead or dying by the wayside." We can see they were Iron Rule people.

There came along a priest, a model of religious zeal; he saw the man, and passed by on the other side. After him came a Levite, a prospective priest; he heard the man sigh or groan, came and looked at him, passed on, dropped into the path, and left the man to die. What rule do these men represent? The Silver Rule. Then there came along the good Samaritan. He heard the groan or sigh, saw the situation, went to the man; bound up his wounds, pouring in oil and wine; led the beast up, put the man upon it, carried him to a house, secured good quarters for him, stayed by and watched him until morning, paid the bill up to that time, and told the host to take care of the sick man, and whatever it cost, he himself would pay it when he came again. What does he represent? The Golden Rule. The Savior approved it, the lawyer approved it, and the Savior said to the lawyer: "Go, and do thou likewise." And all the sons and daughters of the Lord Almighty who have come after have approved it— this principle of the Golden Rule: "All things whatsoever ye would that men should do to you, do ye even so to them."

Now, this is simple, practical Christianity; and when we come short of it, we simply come short of the duties and demands of the religion we profess. When we practice it, it makes us happy and useful, and God will bless us here and hereafter. We ask you to accept a religion of which this is the fundamental principle. And now, if there are any in this audience who are in any sense subjects of the gospel call, any who are desirous of coming out on the Lord's side to cast their lot with his followers, God is willing, Jesus is pleading, mercy is lingering, Heaven is waiting, and all that is necessary is for you to sublimely resolve to abandon sin and Satan, and then carry out that resolution, and God promises you pardon and salvation and blessedness in this life, and everlasting bliss in the home of the soul; and if this be the desire of any or all of you who are subjects of the gospel call, we give you, at the close of this last and final service of the day, a chance to come. Our hearts are pleading with you, our hearts are pleading with the great I Am in your behalf; while the angels who rejoice over one sinner who repents are ready to rejoice with joy unspeakable, if you will only come to Jesus now.

## THE WHOLE DUTY OF MAN

REMEMBER now thy Creator in the days of thy youth, while the evil days come not, nor the years draw nigh, when thou shalt say, I have no pleasure in them (and these dark days are coming to all who do not put their trust in God, and live so as to have the hope of eternal blessings as their light beyond the shadows of time); while the sun, or the light, or the moon, or the stars, be not darkened, nor the clouds return after the rain: in the day when the keepers of the house shall tremble, and the strong men shall bow themselves, and the grinders cease because they are few, and those that look out of the windows be darkened, and the doors shall be shut in the streets, when the sound of the grinding is low, and he shall rise up at the voice of the bird, and all the daughters of music shall be brought low; also when they shall be afraid of that which is high, and fears shall be in the way, and the almond tree shall flourish, and the grasshopper shall be a burden, and desire shall fail; because man goeth to his long home, and the mourners go about the streets, or ever the silver cord be loosed, or the golden bowl be broken, or the pitcher be broken at the fountain, or the wheel broken at the cistern. Then shall the dust return to the earth as it was, and the spirit shall return unto God who gave it.

"Vanity of vanities, saith the preacher; all is vanity." And moreover, because the preacher was wise, he still taught the people knowledge; yea, he gave good heed, and sought out, and set in order many proverbs. The preacher sought to find out acceptable words: and that which was written was upright, even words of truth. The words of the wise are as goads, and as nails fastened by the masters of assemblies, which are given from one shepherd. And further, by these, my son, be admonished: of making many books there is no end; and much study is a weariness of the flesh."

"Let us hear the conclusion of the whole matter: Fear God, and keep his commandments: for this is the whole duty of man. For God shall bring every work into judgment, with every secret thing, whether it be good, or whether it be evil." (Eccles. 12.)

The book called "Ecclesiastes" is a very peculiar book. Of course every book has its distinct peculiarities; and if a book should be made not being peculiar in some respects, it would have no special interest to a literary public, from the fact that its field is already occupied. But Ecclesiastes is a peculiarly peculiar book. It is so exceedingly peculiar that, unless we are careful to understand the general import of it, we may become very greatly bewildered in reading it.

Of all the books that have ever been written, there are exceedingly few that are simpler, plainer, or more easily comprehended than the beautiful book called "Ecclesiastes," and yet there are few books that are harder to comprehend. It is so simple

that little children can understand it from beginning
to end; it is so hard that sages may read from beginning to end and be worse bewildered when they get
through than when they commenced. It depends to
a great extent on your general conception of the
scope, design, and mission of the work as to
whether you understand it immediately, or know
scarcely anything about it at the end of a lifetime of
study. Unquestionably, Solomon, in writing the
book called "Ecclesiastes," was in the hand of
Providence as a great actor upon a stage, with the
universe for an audience, trying to teach all mankind
that this world can never give the bliss for which we
sigh; that it is not the whole of life to live, nor all of
death to die. Now, if we will just take that view of it,
and understand that Solomon is just a great actor,
acting this part now, and not his real self when he is
writing this book, just as Booth, the tragedian, on
the stage presented "Julius Caesar," talking as Julius
Caesar, thinking as Julius Caesar, trying to look like
Julius Caesar, and at the same time being in reality
Booth—now if we can just get this idea, and read
the book with that thought before us, we can
understand it. If you have never read the book with
that key, with that idea, I will feel perfectly safe to
say that you, as honest men and women, would say
that you have never been able to understand
Ecclesiastes; but if you have read it with that key,
that you understand and consider it one of the sim-
plest and sublimest of books.

Man is in quest of happiness in this life. It may be true that "man is made to mourn," as Burns tells us. It is true that "man is born unto trouble, as the sparks fly upward"; for not Burns, but the Bible, tells us that. But it is also true that "man's inhumanity to man makes countless millions mourn," even if Burns, and not the Bible, tells us that. But still, man is in quest of happiness from the cradle to the grave. So if we can see teeming millions tending to a certain point, foraging like bees upon a certain field, or going to drink from a certain fountain, then we can understand that these human beings think that happiness can be found there. This is based upon the fundamental principle of the philosophy of the human mind, and is universally true, always has been true, and always will be true. Now, remembering this, it will not take us very long to see from what source people expect to draw happiness in this life.

There is a widespread, deeply seated, and almost universal impression that knowledge and wisdom can give happiness; hence it is there is a general restlessness in the human family along educational lines. The fathers and mothers are willing to wear their lives away to give their children advantages, many of whom cannot appreciate these sacrifices until they shed unavailing tears above the silent dust of those who gave their lives to lift them up and make them happy. Hence it is that men will trim the midnight lamp, and read, and think, and write, until they sap the very foundation of their physical constitution, and bring themselves to an untimely grave, as Pollock did, many of whose finest writings are in condemnation of that very course, when he was, while writing these things, following that course to a suicide's grave, when otherwise he would have been in the prime and vigor of young manhood. Hence our restlessness with reference to the news. It it is time for the afternoon paper, and we make a mistake and get the morning paper, we are vexed. We want to keep abreast of the times and keep on learning. Now Solomon was the man to go on the stage and present this to all of us, and to go on before us across the stage and then tell us the result.

The curtain rolls up for the first scene and we behold the wise man, Solomon. Look at him. We see he is a marvelous man—the expression of his countenance, the shape of his head, his whole mortal frame bearing the stamp of wisdom and knowledge. He had divine assurance that he was wiser than any man who had preceded him on the stage of action, and until time's knell should sound no man should come upon the stage of action that could rival him. His wisdom was such that kings and queens and princes came from different parts of the earth to study like little children at his feet and gather wisdom from his lips. Amazed and dazzled at the splendor of his wealth of knowledge, they returned to tell their subjects that the half had never been told. We see Solomon on the stage enjoying all his prominence. Is he happy? We see him thinking deeply. We see him take his pen and write, "How dieth the wise man? As the fool"— one event painful to them both; that increase of wisdom is ever an increase of sorrow, and we realize that he is thinking of the day, not far distant, when the flaming torch of his intellectual superiority is to be dipped in the silent river rolling between the shores of time and eternity; that he himself will be upon a level with any toad that dwells in the land, side by side in the solemn silence of death, nor will he have any superiority over the toad when the end comes. So, thus writing, he turns and looks out; we see sorrow and sadness and despair depicted on his face; and he turns and writes: "Vanity and vexation of spirit." In other words, he writes over the fountain of wisdom and knowlege, "All is vanity and vexation of spirit," that the old and young, while time shall last, may read and understand. It means that if you are not looking beyond this world, if you are not looking beyond the stars, but expect to get happiness from the fountain of wisdom and knowlege, you are doomed to disappointment and will find, when the solemn hour of death comes, that "all is vanity and vexation of spirit." And while we see him stand with saddened face, the curtain falls upon the first scene.

There is a widespread impression that wealth can give happiness, that wealth can give the peace for which we sigh. Hence, from the rivers to

the ends of the earth there is a ceaseless struggle—
people trying to gather, to hoard up, wealth. Men
will turn from their loved ones; cross rivers, mountains, plains, and seas; and practically bury themselves alive, in their efforts to gain wealth, as was
illustrated especially back in the early fifties in this
land, when there was a vast army marching from
the older States to the Pacific States to hunt gold in
those golden sands. There are hundreds, if not
thousands, of lonely graves marking forever the
paths that were followed by men in quest of gold.
And people are doing that now. Not many months
ago, just after the train left Louisville, I noticed that
a man on the seat near me was very restless.
Directly he said something to me and we got into a
conversation. He briefly told me his story, and I
learned from him that he was then forty-four years
old; that he had left his old Kentucky home when
he was about twenty-two; that he had gone to the
mining district of Mexico and had spent twenty-
two years there. He was returning home then, with
two bullets in his body and about twenty thousand
dollars in gold in the bank in Louisville for safe-
keeping. He asked the conductor repeatedly about
what time he would get to a certain station. The
conductor could hardly pass without his asking
some question. He said to me: "I am going back
home. I am expecting my brother to meet me there.
Since I left, my father has died, my mother has died,
and my sister also. My brother is still living, and I

expect him to meet me." I said to him: "Now it is all over, and you have given your twenty-two years of life for twenty thousand dollars in gold, do you think it pays?" He thought seriously for a second, and he said: "No, it has not paid. I have money enough, if I will be careful of it, to last me the remainder of my days; but things about the old home have changed, so that as I go back now with the twenty thousand dollars in Louisville to my credit, I cannot be happy." The train stopped; he got off within three miles of his country home. The train simply stopped to let him get off and started on again. I looked back, and the last I saw of him he was in the embrace of a man. I noticed standing near them a boy whom I took to be a nephew. As I went on I thought of the son, that wanderer, going back with his gold, meeting his brother who was left at the old home. He could not ask him: "How is mother? and how is father? and how is sister?" He knew all about that. But he could go back with his brother, and when he got home there was no father to meet him at the gate; there was no mother to come with her arms thrown out to receive him in her fond embrace, to kiss him and sob and weep, and thank God for his return; no sister in the home, keeping the house neat and tidy, and making it a paradise, if possible, because brother was coming home. He could go into the house and see the vacant seats of the absent loved ones; he could go out in the orchard back of it and see the graves of father, mother, and sister, and then remember that he robbed home of the joy and sunshine and gladness with which he might have filled it for twenty-two years. He had left father without a stay and support, mother without his sympathy, and sister without his care, until all had died and he had returned too late to tell them about his fortune and divide his gold with them. As I thought, I did not wonder that the man said, with a sigh: "No, it did not pay." I felt if I had been that man, and had that gold in two packages and could have lifted and thrown them, I would have felt like throwing it all into the depths of the sea. I could not bear to look upon it and think what I had lost and what I had deprived others of in my thirst and search for gold. But this is the history of the world. People have been doing this through all the ages, and there are men who will live like paupers for forty years in order to die rich. Now, then, the race needed someone upon the stage of action for the purpose of presenting this to the human race, to tell us the result before it was too late; for if that man could have looked down the stream of time to the morning when we met for the first, and perhaps for the last, time—could have seen the difference between then and now in his old Kentucky home—he would not have gone to Mexico; he would have stayed at home. The race needed someone to present these things, that we might learn without such bitter experience. While thinking thus, we notice that the curtain has rolled up, and we see the same actor. He has retained his knowledge, his wisdom, his experience, but he is just glittering with radiant gems and jewels rare and with flashing diamonds. As he turns in the light he is perfectly dazzling. We look around him; we see nothing that is less precious than gold—gold and pearls and diamonds—things of wondrous commercial value. We look up the great stage; in the background it seems that the wealth of the universe has been fathered and heaped. And why? Solomon is the richest of the earth. Men experienced along that line, who have made estimates, tell us that Solomon's wealth was such that Croesus, whose name has been a synonym for wealth, was practically a homeless wanderer, a penniless pauper in comparison with him. In Solomon's days the surrounding nations poured their glittering, golden treasures into Palestine, and Solomon had charge of these treasures. Gold and silver were as rocks for abundance about Jerusalem at that time. He realized that his wealth was almost boundless; that it was practically impossible for him, by reckless extravagance, to diminish the wonders of his wealth. Was he happy with all this wealth, with all these streams flowing in perpetually—the streams of glittering gold—dwelling in a palace that caught the rays of the rising sun upon a golden roof? If wealth can make a man happy, Solomon is happy. But he has sense enough to know that he can use but little of this wealth; he can dwell in but one golden palace at a time; he can sleep upon but one couch, wear only one suit of clothes, eat but one meal at a time. He can in a lifetime use very little of his wealth, and he is grieved and burdened and perplexed because of his anxieties with reference to the great surplus he has. He has sense enough to know that he can never use it, and beyond what he can use it cannot practically bless—just as if a man were thirsty, and the Pacific Ocean were the best of water to drink, and he owned it and had it hedged about so that no bird or man or mouse could drink of it. He could drink but a little of it at a time, and all the rest would be practically valueless to him. Then the thought ought to come to him: "It is cruel to have all this ocean when I can drink but a little, and let teeming millions die of thirst in agony. " Then Solomon remembered that he knew not whose these things would be when he departed, whether this wondrous wealth would belong to a wise man or a fool. He did not know whether friends or foes would own it then. He did not know but that the sons for whom he was hoarding up would butcher each other, and stain with blood the very treasures he had spent a lifetime in gathering together. He remembers that if he had owned the whole earth, and owned it until he died, there would be but one breath between the millionaire and the pauper; that the hour was coming when he would die, and one moment after he breathed his last breath he would be as poor as the poorest beggar in the land; that his body would sleep in the bosom of the earth, and that would be all of earth to him; and he turns away in deepest sadness, and writes over that pool—the glittering, golden pool of wealth—"Vanity and vexation of spirit," thus saying to the human race: "If you expect wealth to make you happy, you might as well stop now, for at the end of your race it is all vanity and vexation of spirit." The curtain drops, the scene ends, but the lesson is ours.

We have the same evidence that there is a widespread impression, especially among the young, that revelry, rowdyism, dissipation, frolic, frivolity, and fun can give happiness. There are in this town thousands of hopeless, hapless, helpless invalids languishing upon beds of affliction, who would have been happy fathers and mothers now had they learned in early childhood, and reduced to practice, what all of us may learn from the lesson taught us by Solomon, if we will. Their parents warned them, some of them having probably followed the same course and learned from experience the folly of it, but could not teach them. They thought: "You have had your day and do not want others to be happy." So on they went and wrecked themselves, and others are going on the same way, not taking time to heed the words of warning, but hastening on, thinking they will miss the rocks on which others were wrecked, and so the race goes on. Now, God, taking the place of all anxious, careful parents, has put Solomon on the stage to show us the folly of such a course. While we are thinking of this, the curtain rolls up and there is the actor. The stage is glittering with gems, covered with gold. We can see that Solomon is a man of wealth, but his costume is changed, his appearance is changed. He has retained his wealth, his wisdom, his knowledge, but he is dressed like a rowdy. He reels, and every movement shows that he is just from the giddy dance. The Bible tells us that he gave himself up to mirth; that he procured men singers, and women singers, and gave himself up to the follies of man, and withheld from himself no good thing—that is, what the rowdy calls good. He "went all the gaits," went all the way—does that while he is on the stage before us. Is Solomon happy in the midst of all this? He thinks—for he could not retain his wisdom and not think—he remembers that this cannot last; he remembers that after a night of revelry there is a day of headache, a day of utter gloom and misery; he remembers that after a lifetime of rowdyism there is a night of endless darkness. He remembers that the day is not far distant when the jeweled fingers touching so lightly the harp strings that vibrate and give forth strains of music almost divine are to be cold and stiff as icicles; when the eyes that look tender love into the depths of eyes that look love in return will be closed to earth and all its pleasures; when that throng of revelers, with their laughter and jest and song, will be cold and silent in the bosom of the earth, and but for the oncoming tide of humanity to take the place of the tide that now is, his royal palace would soon be as silent as the chambers of death. In deepest sadness he turns and writes over that whirlpool of pleasure, "Vanity and vexation of spirit"; the curtain falls, and the third scene is ended.

There is an impression in the world that power can give happiness. There is not a crime in the long catalogue of sin too bad for men to commit in order to gain and retain power, as the history of the world clearly shows, reaching down from remotest ages to the present time. The history of the world shows that men will shed blood; that men will convert happy homes into blazing wrecks; that men will drench fertile, peaceful lands with blood and fill them with moans and shrieks of unavailing sorrow, to gain and retain power. They will sacrifice the truest, fondest friends they have, as did Napoleon, who tore from his embrace the pure, faithful, loving wife, as a farmer would dash from his hand a venomous viper, and left her to die of a broken heart, that he might form a matrimonial alliance that would give him a little more power, or help him retain the power he already held. Now, knowing this, God wanted the sons of men to know before it was too late what would be the result of such ambition; and while we are thinking of this, the curtain rolls up, and again we see

Solomon, with his wisdom, his wealth, Solomon relaxed by his revelry, sitting upon an ivory throne, dazzling with radiant splendor, with a crown upon his head such as the world had never seen, with a royal scepter in his hand—Israel's king swaying that scepter over Israel's hosts. In a few seconds of time the space of forty years sweeps by. Solomon is swaying the scepter over proud Israel, a commander in chief, before whose hosts the combined armies of the earth were driven like chaff before the storm king in his fury. Is Solomon happy now? We look and see sadness succeeding the expression of gladness. Solomon is thinking now that this cannot last; that the day is not far distant when the arm that sways that scepter is to be unnerved, and Solomon, the mighty king, will be no more than the beggar in the dust. Like Xerxes, when he looked down upon the marshaled hosts crossing the Hellespont to rob Greece of her glory, and wept to remember that in a hundred years all that host and the sovereign thereof would be silent in the grave, so Solomon knows that a day is coming when Israel's king and Israel's hosts will alike be vanquished by an unseen foe. He turns and writes over that whirlpool of earthly power and glory, "Vanity and vexation of spirit," and the fourth scene is ended forever.

We all know enough of the history of the world to realize something of the vanity and vexation of such ambition. Do we not remember the disappointment of Alexander, who brought himself to a drunkard's grave by debauchery when he was scarcely one-third of a century old, just when he was recognized as the ruler or conqueror of the world? Do we not remember Caesar, wounded by the very men he had loved and treated as friends; Hannibal, who committed suicide in a foreign land? And do we not know enough of these things to realize that the lesson coming from Solomon is a correct one? But the curtain falls, and the scene is ended.

While we are thinking, it rolls up again, and gives us the fifth and last scene. And now when I am done presenting this lesson, and you are done with your patient, polite listening, then you can go home and study and study until God shall call you hence, but you will not find anything that mortals depend upon for happiness that has not been presented in one of these four pictures—in wisdom, in wealth, in pleasure, or in power. The curtain rises and we can see far down the stage. It is a little gloomy, but the mists clear away, and through the rifted clouds the sun shines down, and we can see, far away on the other side of the stage, Solomon again. What is he doing? Weary of these things, he has retired from the busy haunts of men to commune with nature in fair primeval woods, to find the bliss for which the soul sighs. We see that he is looking at a dewdrop that rests on the cheek of a fragrant flower—the tear of night, but now the radiant gem of the morning, in whose bosom the blazing sun is mirrored, a gem equaling in beauty any gem in his diadem. Something attracts his attention—he hears a bird sing, and looks to see it, but the bird is gone. He turns again to the dew-drop, but at the first kiss of morning it has dropped from the cheek of the flower and it is gone. Something attracts his attention—he looks around, and, looking back again, he sees the flower itself is faded; too sensitive and delicate to bear the sunshine upon it, it falls to the earth and the dust has hidden its sweetness and its beauty. He looks again; years have flown by like moments. He sees the tall trees, that stood like bannered hosts in battle array, tottering; the cedars fall—the tall cedars of Lebanon. The hills are crumbling, the mountains are fallen. The nations of the earth sink down into the bosom of death. He turns to the heavens; he sees the stars falling from the withered vault above, it being night because the sun has been suddenly extinguished. The time for the crash of matter and the wreck of worlds is come. He sees the elements melt like wax before the flame. The right arm of Jehovah is bared; he shakes the earth and folds up the firmament like a scroll. The whole world is ablaze, lighting up with fearful splendor the eternal city of our God. It is all gone, and Solomon turns and writes back over the flame: "Vanity and vexation of spirit."

He comes to the front and stands before us. He tells us that he appreciates the privilege and opportunity that God has given him to show the value of earthly things, if we look to them for happiness; and then dipping his pen in the living light of God, he brings it down upon the waiting scroll, and as he writes he breathes it out to all the listening earth: "Let us hear the conclusion of the whole matter: Fear God, and keep his commandments; for this is the whole duty of man. For God shall bring every work into judgment, with every secret thing, whether it be good, or whether it be evil." And having thus written the conclusion of the whole matter, the pen drops from his weary fingers, the curtain falls, the picture is complete, the play is ended.

This is Ecclesiastes. Only in the gift of his Son to save a ruined and recreant race has God manifested more clearly his love for the sons and daughters of men than in placing Solomon upon the stage to teach us these wonderful lessons.

I am here tonight to try in a feeble way to bring these lessons before you. I rejoice that it is my privilege to encourage you, men and women, boys and girls, to come out on the Lord's side. Remember that we are drifting to eternity's sea; that our hearts "Still, like muffled drums, are beating/Funeral marches to the grave."

Remember, there is no more solemn truth than "man no longer begins to live than he begins to die." Remember that we are dying perpetually, but while we are dying the Lord Jesus Christ practically stands before us, in God's eternal truth, wiser than

Solomon, and says to all of you that are subjects of the gospel call: "Come unto me, all ye that labor and are heavy laden, and I will give you rest. Take my yoke upon you, and learn of me; for I am meek and lowly in heart; and ye shall find rest unto your souls. For my yoke is easy, and my burden is light." Jesus practically says: "Poor dying sons and daughters of men, I am your Savior; I, by the grace of God, am your only Savior. I came from the courts of glory to these low grounds of sorrow, lived a life of poverty and pain, and died on the cross, and now I call you to me. If you will live in harmony with my will, my God shall be your God, he will be your shield and exceeding great reward; you shall be holy and happy here and blessed in that deathless land forever." If you believe these things; if you believe the Bible; if you believe the Savior tells you the truth; if you believe the Savior does actually say to you, "Come unto me, all ye that labor and are heavy laden, and I will give you rest"; that he says, "I, Jesus, have sent mine angels to declare unto you that I am the root and offspring of David, the bright and morning star"—if so, may the Lord bless every one of you in rising and coming to Jesus to be saved, while we wait to lovingly welcome you and pray that you may come.

# ENDNOTES

CHAPTER I—HISTORICAL BACKGROUND

1. Winifred E. Garrison and Alfred T. DeGroot, *The Disciples of Christ* (St. Louis: Christian Board of Publications, 1948), p. 21.
2. Matthew 16:18, 19. All Biblical citations refer to the KJV.
3. Galatians 4:4.
4. M. M. Davis, *The Restoration Movement of the Nineteenth Century* (Cincinnati: The Standard Publishing Co., 1913). p. 3.
5. Acts. 2:1-4.
6. George P. Fisher, *History of the Christian Church* (New York: Charles Scribner's Sons, 1915), p. 19.
7. I Corinthians 3:11.
8. Matthew 28:18; II Timothy 3:16, 17.
9. Acts 11:26; I Peter 4:16.
10. I Corinthians 1:2.
11. Romans 16:16.
12. Acts 20:28.

13. Acts 2:47.
14. Ephesians 1:22.
15. Hebrews 12:23.
16. Colossians 1:13.
17. Acts 20:7.
18. Acts 2:42.
19. Acts 2:42.
20. Acts 2:42.
21. I Corinthians 16:2.
22. Colossians 3:16; Ephesians 5:19.
23. Acts 14:23; Philippians 1:1.
24. Matthew 28:18-20; Mark 16:15-16; Luke 24:45-46.
25. John 17:20-21.
26. I Corinthians 1:1.
27. Acts 20:28-30; I Timothy 4:1-3; II Timothy 4:2-4.
28. Fisher, p.99.
29. Preserved Smith, *The Age of the Reformation* (New York: Henry Holt and Co., 1920), p. 115.
30. Williston Walker, *The Reformation* (New York: Charles Scribner's Sons, 1900), p. 463.
31. E. H. Klotsche and J. Theodore Mueller, *The History of Christian Doctrine* (Burlington: The Lutheran Literary Board, 1945), p. 237.
32. William W. Sweet, *The Story of Religions in America* (New York: Harper and Brothers Publishers, 1930), pp. 11-37.
33. Jesse L. Hulbert, *The Story of the Christian Church* (Philadelphia: John C. Winston Co., 1933), p. 176.
34. William Lecky, *A History of England in the Eighteenth Century* (London: Longmans, Green and Co., 1878), I, pp. 74-80.
35. Frederick J. Turner, *The Frontier in American History*, (New York: Henry Holt and Co., 1920), p. 165.
36. Frederick J. Gielow, *Popular Outline of Church History*, (Cincinnati: Standard Publishing Co., 1926), p. 146.
37. Garrison and DeGroot, p. 36.
38. Ibid., pp. 40-45.
39. Earle West, *The Search for the Ancient Order*, (Nashville: Gospel Advocate Co., 1957), I. p. 10.

40. Ibid., p. 22.
41. M.M. Davis, *How the Disciples Began and Grew* (Cincinnati: Standard Publishing Co., 1915), p. 117.
42. West, p. 129.
43. Ibid.

CHAPTER II—BRIGHT PROMISES: T.B. LARIMORE'S EARLY YEARS

1. Mrs. T.B. Larimore, *Life, Letters and Sermons of T. B. Larimore*, (Nashville: Gospel Advocate Co., 1931), p. 7.
2. Ibid.
3. H. Leo Boles, *Biographical Sketches of Gospel Preachers*, (Nashville: Gospel Advocate Co., 1932), p. 333.
4. F.D. Srygley, *Larimore and His Boys*, (Nashville: McQuiddy Printing Co., 1898). p. 58.
5. Ibid., p. 59.
6. Larimore, p. 8
7. Ibid., p. 81.
8. Ibid., p. 87.
9. Srygley, p. 69.
10. Larimore, p. 11.
11. Ibid., p. 14.
12. The original unpublished recommendation is in the possession of the great nephew of T. B. Larimore, W. H. Baldy, Jr., Memphis, Tennessee.
13. James E. Scobey, *Franklin College and Its Influence*, (Nashville: McQuiddy Printing Co., 1906), p. 412.
14. Ibid.
15. Ibid., p. 414.
16. Ibid., p. 411.
17. Srygley, *Larimore and His Boys*, p. 91.
18. Ibid.
19. Ibid., p. 93.
20. Mrs. Larimore, p. 14.
21. Ibid., p. 16.
22. Ibid., p. 17.

CHAPTER III—MATURE YEARS: FAMILY TIES

1. Unpublished letter in possession of the great nephew of
T. B. Larimore, W. H. Baldy, Jr., Memphis, Tennessee.
2. Page, *Letters and Sermons of T. B. Larimore*, II, 364.
3. Srygley, *Larimore and His Boys*, p. 65.
4. Ibid., p. 66.
5. Ibid., p. 67.
6. Page, *Letters and Sermons of T. B. Larimore*, II, 406.
7. Ibid., p. 409.
8. Ibid., III, 135.
9. Ibid., p. 136.
10. Emma Page, *Julia Esther Gresham Larimore*, Gospel
Advocate, XLIX, No. 29 (1907), p. 451.
11. Ibid.
12. Ibid.
12. Page, *Letters and Sermons of T. B. Larimore*, III, p. 147.


CHAPTER IV—MARVELOUS MEETINGS

1. Emma Page, *Letters and Sermons of T.B. Larimore*, (Nashville:
McQuiddy Printing Co., 1904), p. 39.
2. Ibid., p. 42.
3. Ibid., p. 41.
4. Ibid., p. 153.
5. Srygley, *Larimore and His Boys*, pp. 10-11.
6. Ibid., p. 31.
7. Larimore, p. 135.
8. Personal letter from Batsell Barrett Baxter in my files.
9. Personal letter from C. E. W. Dorris in my files.
10. Srygley, *Larimore and His Boys*, p. 60.
11. Page, *Letters and Sermons of T. B. Larimore*, III, p. 53.
12. Srygley, *Letters and Sermons of T. B. Larimore*, pp. 80-81.
13. Larimore, p. 131.
14. Srygley, *Larimore and His Boys*, p. 208.

15. Srygley, *Letters and Sermons of T. B. Larimore*, p. 72.

16. Larimore, p. 31.

17. Page, *Letters and Sermons of T. B. Larimore*, II, p. 135.

18. Larimore, p. 307.

19. Srygley, *Letters and Sermons of T. B. Larimore*, p. 74.

20. J.M. McCaleb, "Missionary," *Gospel Advocate*, LII, No. 10 (1911), p. 295.

21., Srygley, *Larimore and His Boys*, p. 190.

22. Page, *Letters and Sermons of T. B. Larimore*, II, 51.

23. Ibid., p. 57.

24. G.C. Brewer, "Brother Larimore's Influence in My Life," *Gospel Advocate*, LXXI, No. 21 (1929), 482-483.

CHAPTER V—A MAN OF PEACE AND PURITY

1. Page, *Letters and Sermons of T. B. Larimore*, p. 38.

2. Personal letter from S. P. Pittman in my files.

3. F.D. Srygley, *Letters and Sermons of T. B. Larimore*, (Nashville: Gospel Advocate Co., 1900), I, p. 212.

4. Srygley, *Larimore and His Boys*, pp. 12-13.

5. Srygley, *Letters and Sermons of T. B. Larimore*, p. 140.

6. Ibid., p. 127.

7. Ibid., p. 129.

8. Ibid., p. 135.

9. Ibid., p. 322.

10. Page, *Letters and Sermons of T. B. Larimore*, II, p. 183.

11 Ibid., p. 184.

12. Ibid., p. 188.

13. David Lipscomb, "Query Department," *Gospel Advocate*, XLIX, No. 39 (1907), pp. 614-616.

14. J. W. Shepherd, "Miscellany," *Gospel Advocate*, XLIX, No. 42 (1907), p. 661.

15. Srygley, *Letters and Sermons of T. B. Larimore*, pp. 126-127.

16. Ibid., pp. 129-130.

17. Page, *Letters and Sermons of T. B. Larimore*, III, 93, 95.

18. Ibid.

19. Ibid., p. 96.

20. Larimore, p. 339.


CHAPTER VI—HIS LATER YEARS

1. T.B. Larimore letter to Floyd and Chestnut Church, August 20, 1888.
2. N.B. Hardeman, "A Word of Appreciation," *Gospel Advocate*, LXXI, No. 20 (1929), p. 458.
3. Srygley, *Larimore and His Boys*, p. 244.
4. Ibid.
5. Ibid., p. 245.
6. Interview with Mr. and Mrs. Barnes at Monteagle, Tennessee, February 2, 1960.
7. Larimore, *Letters and Sermons of T. B. Larimore*, pp. 20-21.
8. W.S. Long, "Brother Larimore's Work in Washington," *Gospel Advocate*, LXI, No. 20 (1929), p. 472.
9. Larimore, *Letters and Sermons of T. B. Larimore*, p.22.
10. Original telegram in possession of W.H. Baldy, Jr.
11. F.L. Rowe, "My Personal Acquaintance," *Gospel Advocate*, LXXI, No. 20 (1929), p. 473.
12. Mrs. T.B. Larimore, "Details of Brother Larimore's Passing," *Gospel Advocate*, LXXI (1929), p. 465.


CHAPTER VII—CONTEMPORARY APPRAISALS OF T.B. LARIMORE

1. F.C. Sowell, "T.B. Larimore and E. A. Elam," *Gospel Advocate*, LXXI, No. 21 (1929), p. 498.
2. C.L. Wilkinson, "He 'Yet Speaketh!'", *Gospel Advocate*, LXXI, No. 20 (1929), p. 495.
3. Ernest Beam, "The Gravity of T.B. Larimore," *Gospel Advocate*, LXXI, No. 20 (1929), p. 486.
4. E.C. Fuqua, "Triumphant T B. Larimore," *Gospel Advocate*, LXXI, No. 20 (1929), p. 485.
5. E.N. Glen, "As I Knew Brother Larimore," *Gospel Advocate*, LXI, No. 20 (1929), p. 485.

6. F.W. Smith, "What T.B. Larimore Was to Me," *Gospel Advocate*, LXXI, No. 20 (1929), p. 470.

7. A.G. Freed, "T.B. Larimore—A Teacher," *Gospel Advocate*, LXXI, No. 20 (1929), p. 461.

8. M.C. Kurfees, "The Departure of T.B. Larimore," *Gospel Advocate*, LXXI, No. 20 (1929), p. 460.

9. F.L. Rowe, "My Personal Acquaintance," *Gospel Advocate*, LXXI, No. 20 (1929), p. 473.

10. Wayne W. Burton, "Unique Career in Church History," *Gospel Advocate*, LXXI, No. 20 (1929), pp. 475-476.

11.*Nashville Banner*, "Noted Divine Answers Call," reprinted in *Gospel Advocate*, LXXI, No. 20 (1929), p. 478.

12. Larimore, *Letters and Sermons of T. B. Larimore*, p. 155.

13. Personal letter from S. P. Pittman in my files.

## CONCLUSION

1. Paul Southern, *Christian Discipleship*, Abilene Christian Lectures, Austin: Firm Foundation Publishing House, 1938, p. 115.

2. Page, *Letters and Sermons of T. B. Larimore*, III, p. 155.

3. Ibid., p. 159.

# BIBLIOGRAPHY

**BOOKS**

American Standard Version of the Bible.

Boles, H. Leo. *Biographical Sketches of Gospel Preachers.* Nashville: Gospel Advocate Co., 1932.

Davis, M. M. *How the Disciples Began and Grew.* Cincinnati: Standard Publishing Co., 1915.

---. *The Restoration Movement of the Nineteenth Century.* Cincinnati: The Standard Publishing Co., 1913.

Fisher, George P. *History of the Christian Church.* New York: Charles Scribner's Sons, 1915.

Garrison, Winifred E., and Alfred T. DeGroot. *The Disciples of Christ.* St. Louis: Christian Board of Publication, 1948.

Gielow, Frederick J. *Popular Outline of Church History.* Cincinnati: Standard Publishing Co., 1926.

Hurlbert, Jesse L. *The Story of the Christian Church.* Philadelphia: John C. Winston Co., 1933.

Klotsche, E.H., and J. Theodore Mueller. *The History of Christian Doctrine.* Burlington: The Lutheran Literary Board, 1945.

Larimore, Emma Page. *Our Corner Book.* Nashville: Publishing House of the M.E. Church, South, 1912.

Larimore, Mrs. T.B. *Letters and Sermons of T. B. Larimore.* Nashville: Gospel Advocate Co., 1931.

Lacky, William E.H. *A History of England in the Eighteenth Century* I. London: Longmans, Green and Co., 1878.

Page, Emma. *Letters and Sermons of T. B. Larimore.* Nashville: McQuiddy Printing Co., 1904.

Scobey, James E. Franklin *College and Its Influence.* Nashville: McQuiddy Printing Co., 1906.

Smith, Preserved. *The Age of the Reformation.* New York: Henry Holt and Co., 1920

Southern, Paul. *The Mind of Christ, Abilene Christian College Bible Lectures 1938.* Austin: Firm Foundation Publishing House, 1939.

Srygley, F.D. *Larimore and His Boys.* Nashville: McQuiddy Printing Co., 1898.

---. *Letters and Sermons of T.B. Larimore.* Nashville: Gospel Advocate Co., 1900.

Sweet, William W. *The Story of Religions in America.* New York: Harper and Brothers Publishers, 1930.

Thonssen, Lester, and A. Craig Baird. *Speech Criticism.* New York: The Ronald Press, 1948.

Turner, Frederick J. *The Frontier in American History.* New York: Henry Holt and Co., 1920.

Walker, Williston. *The Reformation.* New York: Charles Scribner's Sons, 1900.

West, Earle. *The Search for the Ancient Order. I.* Nashville: Gospel Advocate Co., 1957.


PERIODICALS

Beam, Ernest. "The Gravity of T.B. Larimore." *Gospel Advocate,* LXXI, No. 20 (May 1929), 494.

Brewer, G.C. "Brother Larimore's Influence in My Life." *Gospel Advocate,* LXXI, No. 21 (May 1929), 482, 483.

Burton, Wayne W. "Unique Career in Church History." *Gospel Advocate,* LXXI, No. 20, (May 1929), 475, 476.

Freed, A.G. "T.B. Larimore—A Teacher." *Gospel Advocate,* LXXI, No. 20 (May 1929), 461.

Fuqua, E.C. "Triumphant T.B. Larimore." *Gospel Advocate,* LXXI, No. 20 (May 1929), 486.

Glen, E.N. "As I Knew Brother Larimore." *Gospel Advocate,* LXXI, No. 20 (May 1929), 485.

Kurfees, M.C. "The Departure of T.B. Larimore." *Gospel Advocate,* LXXI, No. 20 (May 1929), 460.

Larimore, Mrs. T.B. "Details of Brother Larimore's Passing." *Gospel Advocate*, LXXI, No. 20 (May 1929), 465.

Lipscomb, David. "Query Department." *Gospel Advocate*, XLIX, No. 39 (September 1907), 614, 616.

Hardeman, N.B. "A Word of Appreciation." *Gospel Advocate*, LXXI, No. 20 (May 1929), 458.

Long, W.S. "Brother Larimore's Work in Washington." *Gospel Advocate*, LXXI, No. 20 (May 1929), 472.

McCaleb, J.M. "Missionary." *Gospel Advocate*, LIII, No. 10 (March 1911), 295.

*Nashville Banner*. "Noted Divine Answers Call." reprint in *Gospel Advocate*, LXXI, No. 20 (May 1929), 478.

Page, Emma. "Julia Esther Gresham Larimore." *Gospel Advocate*, XLIX, No. 29 (July 1907), 451.

Rowe, F.L. "My Personal Acquaintance." *Gospel Advocate*, LXXI, No. 20 (May 1929), 473.

Shepherd, J.W. "Miscellany." *Gospel Advocate*, XLIX, No. 42 (October 1907), 661.

Smith, F.W. "What T.B. Larimore was to Me." *Gospel Advocate*, LXXI, No. 20 (May 1929), 470.

Sowell, F.C. "T. B. Larimore and E.A. Elam." *Gospel Advocate*, LXXI, No. 21 (May 1929), 498.

Wilkerson, C.L. "He 'Yet Speaketh.'" *Gospel Advocate*, LXXI, No. 20 (May 1929), 495.

## PERSONAL INTERVIEWS AND UNPUBLISHED LETTERS

Unpublished recommendation as a teacher in the possession of Mr. W.H. Baldy, Jr., Memphis, Tennessee.

Unpublished personal letter in possession of Mr. W.H. Baldy, Jr., Memphis, Tennessee

Unpublished telegram in possession of Mr. W.H. Baldy, Jr., Memphis, Tennessee.

Personal interview with Mr. and Mrs. Barnes, Monteagle, Tennessee, February 2, 1960.

Personal letter from Batsell Barrett Baxter.

Personal letter from C.E.W. Dorris.

Personal letters from S.P. Pittman.